SINS
OF THE
FATHER

SINS
OF THE
FATHER

MARIANNE MORRIS

Pacific Press Publishing Association
Boise, Idaho
Oshawa, Ontario, Canada

Edited by David C. Jarnes
Designed by Dennis Ferree
Cover photo by Stan Sinclair
Typeset in 10/12 New Century Schoolbook

Library of Congress Cataloging-in-Publication Data:

Morris, Marianne, 1951-   .
        Sins of the Father / Marianne Morris.
              p.   cm.
        ISBN 0-8163-1146-3
        1. Child molesting—United States—Case studies. 2. Child
molesters—United States—Family relationships—Case
studies. I. Title.
        HV6570.2.M67   1993
        364.1'536...dc20   92-42184
                                                                                CIP

93 94 95 96 97 ● 5 4 3 2 1

Contents

Preface

Sex abuse perpetrated by a "Christian" causes greater damage than that done by any other person. Not only can such abuse distort the victim's perception of God, but it can also cause the victim to distrust anything or anyone religious.

This is the story of one family, and through that family, of the way child abuse by a "Christian" can reverberate through generation after generation—the "ever after" that child-abuse victims and the wider circle of people whose lives touch theirs have to deal with.

My name is not really Marianne Morris, and I have not used the actual names of any of the other people in this book. I am still keeping secrets for the family whose story I am telling. The book portrays many of the events described as taking place in a Crescent City, California, church. That is not the actual scene of these events. And the laws discussed in this story are not the laws of California; the statutes of limitations, laws, and penalties that apply to child abuse vary from state to state. But although I have altered the identities and circumstances of people and places to protect their privacy, this most certainly is a true story.

I have raised and attempted to answer several questions through this story. Which is the truly Christian thing to do: To expose molesters early on, calling them to repentance, offering support to their victims, and preventing further abuses from occurring? Or to protect them at the expense of their victims? Which approach is more helpful to molesters? To their victims?

If you, dear reader, are the victim of sex abuse by someone within your church, and if that abuse has seriously affected your relationship with God, it is my prayer that this story will help you find a warm and trusting relationship with the God whom that person misrepresented to you.

Marianne Morris
March 1993

Characters

Molly (Spencer) Bowker
Steve Bowker—Molly's husband
Teddy (Ted)—Molly and Steve's elder son
Jerry—their second son

Bradley (Brad) and Kate Spencer—Molly's parents
Linda—Molly's sister
Kevin—Linda's husband
Brittany—Linda and Kevin's daughter

Vicki and Leona—Molly's college roommates (They're from
                Crescent City, where Steve's parents live.)

Lloyd and Barbara Bowker—Steve's parents
Patti—Steve's sister
Roger—Patti's husband
Chad and Christopher—Steve's brothers (twins)
Paige—Chad's wife
Megan—Chad and Paige's daughter

Grandpa and Grandma Bowker—Lloyd's parents
Grandpa and Grandma Feldman—Barbara's parents
Louise and Vera—Barbara's sisters

CHAPTER

1

September 1967

Summer cicadas screeched softly in the warm summer after-noon as a gentle wind tousled the uppermost branches of the ancient oak trees on campus. Nervously, Molly Spencer hoisted her overnight bag from the trunk of the blue Buick Skylark and followed her parents to the college dorm. She was uneasy about living away from home. But, remembering her mother's tears from the night before, Molly had decided to be strong. Forcing a smile on her face, she found a surprising sense of delightful anticipation in spite of gnawing anxiety.

The freshmen girls' dormitory looked primeval. At one time it must have been white, as the chipping paint along the corners revealed. Now it seemed more like a faded cream. Three stories tall, the sight of it from the bottom of the wide stairs was humbling. It seemed to snag the clouds that bounced along in the pale blue sky like runaway balloons. Overgrown holly bushes with glossy leaves stood like sentinels beside the turned posts at the foot of the steps.

Molly's father, Bradley, glided up the steps easily, his arms loaded with suitcases and tote bags in several shapes and colors. Molly watched him proudly and again admired, as she always did, how he had kept himself trim and in good physical shape even at the ripe old age of forty-four.

The steps led up grandly to a wide porch with two sets of dark French doors. At the far left, a porch swing swayed in the wind. The doors beside it were open, and through them the warm smell of fried eggs and french fries beckoned. A low murmur of voices, the clatter of silverware, and the clap of trays being stacked drifted onto the porch.

"That must be the cafeteria," Brad told his daughter unnecessarily, and she nodded. Her mother, Kate, joined them, and they scanned the room quietly from the door, then moved to the sparkling French doors beside the cafeteria and entered the dorm lobby.

It was a warm, nostalgic lobby, like something out of a movie. Dark red mahogany door frames matched the solid, polished banister and the wainscoting along the walls. A crimson fringed rug lay on the floor in front of the sweeping stairs, threadbare in places from the thousands of feet that had pounded over it day and night through the years. To the right, an opening had been cut into the wall and surfaced with marble to serve as a reception desk. Behind this counter, the monitor was busy with the day's mail, sorting it into the mailboxes to the left of the desk. She was a stringy-looking girl with green, gooseberry eyes. No doubt her long, brown hair had been caught up in a ponytail earlier that day; but now, long strands hung around her face and over her eyes. One piece was hooked to her eyelash and bobbed up and down when she blinked.

The hallway passed in front of the mailboxes and led through glass doors into a large, oak-floored sitting room furnished with palms and plump, pastel couches. A few enamored couples sat there, visiting quietly.

Kate glanced up at the heavy chandelier in the ceiling and swallowed hard. "I can't believe my little girl is actually in college already," she said. "All the dreams we've shared about your future are actually coming true."

"I was thinking the same thing," Brad admitted. "Where have the years gone?"

Kate adjusted her bulging gray purse from one arm to the other. With more eagerness in her voice than she actually felt, she asked Molly, "What's your room number?"

"I can't remember," Molly replied with an embarrassed grimace.

Kate nodded in the direction of the girl sorting the mail. "Shall we ask her?"

When they asked, the girl looked up somewhat carelessly. "Molly Spencer?" She picked up a dirty clipboard and consulted a paper with curling edges. "You're in room 222," she said, "straight up the stairs, and turn left. It's the first door."

"Thank you." They found the room easily and discovered that two other girls, Vicki Smythe and Leona Miller, had already been assigned to it. The girls were busy setting the room in order, and they froze in surprise when Molly announced she was joining them.

"We've been planning to room together since we were freshmen in high school," the girls told her. "We even bought curtains and bedspreads together."

Molly, noticing that the ruffled curtains were pink, said tactfully, "My bedspread's pink." After a pause, she allowed them a graceful way out. "But if you don't think it's the right shade, I'll just keep my white blanket on top and get pink pillows."

Vicki stuck out her hand and walked over to Molly, swinging her hair out of her eyes. "Hey, no sweat. It's OK. The color scheme's not that important. It's nice to meet you."

Leona observed them without moving, and Molly felt a chill in the air. Excusing herself, Leona brushed past Molly and her parents and hurried down the stairs to the lobby. With a quick wave and a worried frown, Vicki followed on her heels.

"I don't think Leona's very happy to meet me," Molly murmured, busying herself with unpacking.

Her mother said, "She'll warm up eventually."

Molly lifted a grape-colored mohair sweater out of her suitcase and hugged it to her. It was one of the many treasures her mother had found for her at Goodwill, and it had quickly become one of her favorites. "What would I do without parents like you?" she said, meaning it. She knew that on her father's slim salary as a pastor, it was difficult eking out college payments for her and her older sister, Linda—who was attending a college in Michigan. But her parents had insisted that they go to a church college. "We want you to meet Christian young men and marry into good families," they had said. "It's more likely you'll have a happy future if you marry someone you meet on a Christian campus."

Now Kate was blinking back tears.

"No tears today, Mom," Molly said, reminding her of their agreement.

"No tears," her mother agreed with a nod.

Too soon, the suitcases were unpacked, and it was time for prayer and tearful goodbyes. Molly walked her parents back to their car and waved for as long as she could see them, till they rounded a corner and disappeared from sight. In that moment, loneliness seemed to crush her. She felt as insignificant and invisible as a tiny ant as she made her way past clumps of people she didn't know who didn't seem to notice her. She knew nobody! But this was the closest Christian college that offered a two-year medical secretary course, so here she was. It was her choice; she shouldn't wallow in self-pity.

The stairs swam before her, but somehow she lifted one foot after the other and found her way to the bathroom. She was sure nobody would interrupt what she had to do. Her choice or not, she was lonely. She needed a good, cleansing cry.

When Molly awoke the next morning, the room was awash in creamy, yellow light. Seeing her roommates still asleep, she slipped quietly into her jade-green tent dress. She loved its black velvet collar and the long pleat in the back that started at the shoulders and was bisected by a sewn-on belt. It was comfortable, and she felt good in it. She hoped it would help her make a good first impression.

Brushing her straight, auburn hair from her face, she suddenly noticed that Vicki was watching her in the mirror.

"Oh, hi! You're awake!" Molly exclaimed with a laugh.

"If you'll give me a minute," Vicki responded, "I'll wake Leona, and we can eat breakfast together."

"Thanks! I'd like that."

The cafeteria was warm, its atmosphere fragrant with the familiar smells of a country breakfast. "Let's sit in the middle," Vicki said. "We can see the whole cafeteria from there, and I'll introduce you to the kids we know as they pass by."

Leona clearly did not enjoy sharing her friend with Molly. But Vicki was having a good time. Before Molly had finished her scrambled eggs and potatoes, Vicki had introduced her to eight of her friends. Already Molly felt more at home.

Then, as Molly lifted her glass of orange juice to her lips, Vicki let out a gasp that nearly made Molly choke. "What's wrong?" she managed to ask.

"He's here! Look! Over there. See the guy coming in the door? The blond one with the blue jeans and cardigan sweater?"

"He's cute," Molly observed.

"Cute to boot and unattached. You've got to meet him." Vicki stood to her feet and waved, and the boy returned the greeting and made his way through the tables to theirs.

"Hey, Vick. Good to see you!" he said, punching her arm.

Vicki said, "I didn't know you were coming. I thought you were going to work with your dad."

"I was, but Mom talked him into letting me come here instead. Thought I'd give it a try."

"What are you taking?"

"I don't know. General stuff. And you?"

"Same." With a graceful sweep of her hand, Vicki gestured toward Molly. "My roommate here is going to be a medical secretary."

"A secretary, huh?" Steve looked down at her, and the corners of his eyes crinkled warmly. "How fast can you type?"

"Fast enough," Molly said modestly. She smiled confidently, her dark eyes twinkling in a frame of auburn hair. "Nice to meet you. I'm Molly Spencer, and you're—?"

"Steve Bowker."

"I'm sorry," Vicki said, "I should have introduced you. Steve. Molly."

"Is that 'Broker'?" Molly asked, wanting to be sure she said it right.

"No. Bowker. Bow-ker," Steve explained. "Like a bow in your hair."

Molly laughed self-consciously, and Vicki cut in. "Don't worry. He's been through this before. Happens all the time, doesn't it, Steve?"

"Yeah. Someday I'll probably break down and change my name to 'Broker' to make life easier on everybody." He paused, seeming uncomfortable with such personal conversation. "So you're roommates?" he asked, bringing the topic back around to Molly. "Fortunately," Molly replied, "Vicki seems to know everybody; I only know people she's introduced me to."

"Where are you from?"

"I'm from Idaho."

"I see." Steve seemed charmed by her confidence. "Well, maybe we'll have a few classes together, and we can get to know each other better."

"Maybe so," Molly agreed.

"Did you get that job with the choir?" Vicki cut in. "I saw it posted when I registered and thought of you."

Steve nodded. "I saw it too, and got it—fortunately."

"What job is that?" Molly asked.

"I'll be accompanist and reader for the choir director, Dr. Fitzgerald."

"I'm impressed," Molly said with a smile. She was surprised at the wonderful warm feelings this handsome man had stirred up inside. "Maybe I'll see you there. I'm taking choir as an elective."

Steve seemed happy to hear that.

Vicki told her, "He's really good."

"Aw, it's nothing," he said with a wave of his hand. He pushed up the cuff of his sleeve to look at his watch, revealing a tanned, muscular arm. "Oh, look at the time! I gotta run. See you later. Molly, nice to meet you. 'Bye, Leona. Sleepy this morning?"

"She'll wake up eventually," Vicki said lightly.

Molly nodded and gave a small wave.

When Steve was out of earshot, Molly said, "He *is* cute." She was unable to stop smiling as she watched him leave the cafeteria, admiring the square cut of his hairline just above his shirt collar and the natural wave of honey-colored hair at his temples.

"His dad's weird," Leona said dryly. "My folks went to school with his folks—right here. He's probably like his dad; thinks he knows everything."

"Leona—" Vicki began, but Molly cut in, "That's OK. I don't have to date his dad. What kind of work does his dad do?"

Leona answered, "He's a landscaper. My folks said he used

to be a teacher. But when he was fresh out of college, he sort of got into trouble with some kids . . . and kind of lost his job. So he started up his own business."

"What kind of trouble are you talking about?" Molly wondered. She found it difficult to believe that a person as cultured and nice looking as Steve Bowker could have creepy parents.

Leona fixed Molly with a cold stare. "We're talking touchy-feely kind of trouble," she said, raising her eyebrows, "if you know what I mean."

"Leona!" Vicki reprimanded her firmly. "That's just mean gossip. The Bowkers are classic 'pillars in the church.' They hold church office. They attend faithfully. They're at every church picnic and rummage sale. Sometimes they keep little kids at their home on weekends so the parents can get away. They've even provided all the flowers for the Mother's Day service. Everyone loves them." She paused as though searching for more ammunition. "I'd like to know how many other families reach out to others as much as they do!"

Leona shrugged. "Well, your folks haven't known the Bowkers as long as my folks have. My mom said to watch out for him. And I have." She turned to Molly. "Don't say I didn't warn you."

"Thanks," Molly said, suddenly feeling a little uncomfortable—not with Steve's family but with Leona's. What bothered her the most was that Leona's parents would hold a grudge against the man for so many years. It didn't speak highly of them. His "trespasses" must not have been all that bad if he was allowed to hold church office and was held in such high esteem by Vicki and her parents and other members in the church. Molly still wasn't sure what kind of a family Leona came from; perhaps there was some long-standing feud between her parents and Steve's that fueled this undercurrent of slander. It seemed impossible that Steve's family was anything but first rate.

The girls finished eating, returned their trays to the carts, and hurried upstairs to prepare for their first classes. While Leona was in the bathroom and Molly was alone with Vicki, she remarked to Vicki's reflection in the mirror, "Steve seems so nice. Do you really think his family is odd?"

"I think Leona's jealous of his attraction to you, is what I think," Vicki replied. "Steve has a tendency to be arrogant at times—like his father—but not too seriously. I think it's just nervousness that prompts it—or 'older brother syndrome.' He's got a sister a couple of years younger than he is and twin brothers in the lower grades. But I think he's neat. And he's going to break a few hearts."

"What do you mean?"

"I can name at least five girls who are going to flip when they see he's here. They've been trying to catch his eye since he came to our school a year ago, but he hasn't seemed to notice. I think it's too late for them, though. You've snagged him already."

"Oh, come on. He doesn't even know me." Molly forced a light laugh, hoping Vicki's words were true.

"He doesn't know you—yet," Vicki said. "You just wait. I know a look in a man's eye when I see it."

The morning passed quickly. Molly ate lunch alone. As five o'clock neared, she found her palms beginning to sweat and her heart pounding at intervals as she thought about seeing Steve again. This is silly, she told herself. It's just a choir, and he just plays the piano. I don't even know him, for Pete's sake. The thought that there were at least five other girls on campus whom he already knew and who wanted his attentions made her stop her daydreaming. He knows them; he doesn't know me. Besides, I've never had a boyfriend before. What chance do I have? He was just being polite.

A sudden, late-summer squall burst upon the campus during Molly's last class before choir, turning the sky to slate and saturating the flower beds. When she glanced out the window, her heart felt for the rows and rows of cavorting flowers, their heads bent against the torrent. It was still raining when the class was over. But, as she dashed across campus to the music building, it was Molly's head that was bending against the rain.

By the time she got there, she was drenched. Her shoes made squishing noises as she walked down the hall to the bathroom for a quick pick-me-up. Making a face in the mirror, she realized there was little she could do to make herself look better. Her hair was plastered against her face in strings that resembled the yarn hair on a rag doll. Pulling her dress away from her skin, she attempted to dry it, fluttering it against her chest with her fingertips, but it was useless. Molly hoped everyone else in the choir had been caught by the storm too and looked as bedraggled as she did. She sloshed down the hall and entered the choir room, feeling as conspicuous as a mouse on stage at a convention of cats.

It took a few minutes for Dr. Fitzgerald to take roll and divide everyone by parts. "Would those of you who think you sing soprano or tenor please take your places on my left, and those who sing alto or bass over here." He directed the latter group to his right.

Molly moved to the far end of the front row of altos, her shoes making embarrassing sucking noises as she did so. From where she sat, she had a direct view of Steve's face at the piano across the room. She glanced over at him, and her heart skipped a beat when she realized he was watching her. A slow grin spread over his face. He winked charmingly. Smiling self-consciously, Molly looked down and ran her fingers through her hair, pushing it back from her face. Dr. Fitzgerald handed her a clipboard and announced that each person was to sign in. She did so and then took the stack of music he gave her, feeling relieved for the distraction. She took one copy of each piece of music and passed the stack on.

The practice began. First a run-through, to find the difficult parts. Molly's heart swelled with admiration as Steve's skilled fingers brought life to the music. His was a rare talent, there was no doubt. No wonder so many girls wanted to be his "special one." Molly wanted the music to go on and on, but Dr. Fitzgerald insisted they learn their parts section by section, so Steve lined out the parts one note at a time. Whenever Molly's eyes roamed over to his, he caught her glance, and his own eyes warmed. The electricity that only they felt shot across the room.

The rehearsal was over too soon. Molly stayed in her chair to allow Steve the freedom of leaving with whomever he wanted to. When Dr. Fitzgerald began going over some papers with Steve, Molly decided it was safe to leave. She hurried to the door and out into the hall, noting with dismay that it was still raining. Taking a big breath, she was working up the courage to make a dash for the dorm when she felt a tug on her belt. Instinctively, she put a hand to her waist to find who or what was holding her, and a warm hand surrounded hers. She turned to look behind her. Steve had her right hand in one of his, the crook of his umbrella in her belt.

"I seem to be hooked on you," he said with a smile. "Mind if I walk you home?"

Molly let out a laugh. "Oh, you've got an umbrella. Thanks! I'd love to be walked home."

Steve pushed the door with one strong arm, popping his umbrella open as the door swung out. He held out his arm, and Molly took it, breathing deeply the lemony scent of his cologne. He was warm and strong, and she felt very protected. It seemed they were in a magical world of their own.

CHAPTER

2

September 1967

Sitting at the piano, Steve had been watching the door for
Molly's entrance. When he saw her sneak in, his heart gave
a leap. She looked so vulnerable in her wet dress, which at
breakfast had been so stunning on her. Her dark hair clung to her
head and curled under her chin, giving her face a heart-shaped
frame. He heard the slosh of her shoes and felt sorry for her.
The "natives," familiar with the weather, had known the need of
carrying umbrellas. Steve admired Molly's courage in entering
the room and taking a seat on the very front row at the risk of
looking ridiculous.

He thought her too good to be true. He was sure that her
friendship would make this year pass quickly. But Steve also
felt a sense of urgency. On other occasions he had been attracted
to girls he met at school, but being somewhat shy, he had let
half the year pass before revealing his feelings for them. Then
they'd had little time to enjoy their friendship before the school
year ended. Now, here he was at college, and already he had met
the girl of his dreams—a woman with self-confidence and good
looks. If he played this right, perhaps she would be the one to
free him from his family. . . . Maybe they could marry at the end
of the year.

Steve found it difficult to concentrate on the music. And yet
with the heightened sensations Molly's presence had brought,
he felt the emotion of the music more than he ever had before.
The swells and cadences seemed to speak to him, and he played
as though they carried a sweet message to Molly. After enjoying

these heights, playing one note at a time as the sections of the choir worked on their parts was difficult. But it allowed him to glance at her and to catch her looking at him when she thought he wasn't looking. He hoped in the worst way possible that she didn't have a boyfriend back home.

Then the class was over, and Dr. Fitzgerald was calling him. "Here's the clipboard I passed around today. Would you list the people who sing each part?"

"Right now?" Steve's heart fell. He had wanted to walk Molly to the cafeteria for supper. She had waited a few minutes for the others to leave, and now she was heading for the door. If he didn't hurry, he would miss her. Without an umbrella she would get soaked again—might even get sick and have to miss class.

"You don't have to do it now," Dr. Fitzgerald said, shaking his wild mop of white hair. "Sometime tonight. Return it to me tomorrow."

"Oh. OK. Sure. See you." Steve scooted the piano bench back noisily, picked up his umbrella and books, and hurried from the room. With relief he saw that Molly was still at the door, staring at the rain, her shoulders slumped as though defeated. With the crook of his umbrella he hooked the belt at the back of her dress. The look of surprise he saw when she turned around to face him brought a smile to his face.

Back in his room that evening, he organized the list as Dr. Fitzgerald had requested, tracing Molly's name with his fingertips. She had beautiful handwriting. The letters were carefully formed and feminine, and yet they showed a sort of lighthearted carefreeness. "Molly Spencer"—a face he would remember, a name he wanted to change to his.

By the middle of October, Steve had claimed Molly as his special girl. They were going steady, their watches turned under to show they were "taken." They spent long afternoons in the dormitory parlor, visiting. It was during one of these visits that Molly brought up the subject of the talent show coming up in six weeks—right after Thanksgiving.

"You should play a piano solo, Steve."

"I dunno. I'm not that good."

"Oh, yes, you are! You're fantastic!"

His arm was around her shoulder, and he pulled her toward him. "I'll bet you say that to all the guys."

"No. And there haven't *been* any other guys—you know that. You're a top-notch piano player—Vicki told me you won grand prize last year at your school; I'll bet you could win the grand prize here! I really think you should play." Molly raised her eyebrows and cocked her head, pursing her lips. "So it's settled. And I'm marching down right now and putting your name in for the auditions." She struggled out from under his arm and stood to her feet with a gamine grin, daring him to follow. "Well, are you coming or not?"

"OK, OK. I'm coming. But you've got to do something too."

"I am. Vicki and a bunch of us are doing a short skit."

Steve followed Molly to the student association building without saying a word, his large hand swinging her slender one as they walked. After they had turned in his name, Steve became unusually somber and withdrawn.

Molly stopped him and studied his face in the yellow light of the hall. "What's the matter?"

"Nothing."

"Oh, yes, there is. What's the matter with you? Why are you so sad?"

"I'm not sad." He faced her. "I really hate performing, Molly."

"But you're so good at it!"

Steve shook his head. "Playing for the choir is a lot different from playing for a performance."

"This isn't a performance; it's a fun talent show."

"It's not fun when you know that if you make a mistake, you'll hate yourself."

"You don't have to hate yourself," she said with a quizzical smile, uncertain whether to take him seriously.

"But I do hate myself when I goof. What's the use of playing if you don't do your best? To do anything less is shameful."

"I can't believe you're saying this," Molly exclaimed. Crossing her arms over her chest and stamping one foot on the floor, she playfully ordered, "Come on—snap out of it. It's just a fun little program, and everyone's going to enjoy your part." Then, seeing the very real fear in Steve's eyes, she softened. "Steve, if you really don't want to do this, you don't have to. We can go back and tell them you changed your mind."

"No, I'll do it. But I won't enjoy it."

"Maybe you'll surprise yourself," Molly said.

Molly and Steve passed the auditions for the program and began practicing fiercely. Both sets of parents were planning on attending the talent show. While Molly was curious about Steve's parents, her shyness made her dread meeting them.

The evening of the program, Molly's confidence just about disappeared. She even found dressing a difficult task. "Where's my deodorant?" she muttered to Vicki, randomly opening and closing the cupboards under the sink.

Vicki was pulling on a navy blue sweat shirt. "It's on the counter," she said, the fabric muffling her voice.

"That's not my deodorant; that's my hairsp—" Molly reached for the can she had just used on her hair. "Oh, no! It *is* deodorant! Vicki! I just sprayed deodorant on my hair!"

"You what?" Vicki had her head out now.

"I sprayed deodorant on my hair! I can't believe this. I didn't know I was so nervous."

"It's just a little part in a skit," Vicki reminded her.

"I know. But afterwards I have to meet Steve's parents." She paused. "At least my hair won't be sweaty!" She giggled at her own joke. Then she turned serious. "Do you think they'll like me?"

"Why shouldn't they?"

"I don't know. Steve's so good looking, they're probably aristocrats, and I'm just . . . well . . . common."

"Not to Steve."

"I know. Isn't he something?"

"Come on," Vicki prodded her. "His parents are just normal people. Use the real hairspray, and let's get going. I don't want to be late."

Molly didn't know exactly where her parents were sitting, but she knew that wherever they were, they were beaming at her. They never missed a program either of their girls were in. Somehow, knowing they were out there in the dark, murmuring crowd gave Molly the boost she needed to do her best. Her part tonight was one of the funniest she had ever had; she was sure her parents would love it.

The house lights dimmed, and the program began. Waiting with Molly backstage, Steve paced nervously, humming his piano solo over and over.

Molly patted the chair beside her. "Come on—sit down! Relax! It's just a talent show; it isn't the Olympics."

Steve was unusually gruff. "Maybe to you it isn't," he said, "but I can't afford to make a mistake."

"No one's going to shoot you," Molly said good-naturedly, trying to calm him down.

"Good as."

"What do you mean?"

"I can't make a mistake, Molly. I'll hate myself."

"But you don't need to hate yourself if you do your best."

"Whatever I do reflects on my family. I've got their reputation to protect. They've come to every single concert or performance I've been in. They've got miles and miles of tape of just me. I've got to do well. If I blow it . . . I don't know . . . I just can't make a mistake." He slammed one fist into the palm of his hand and then held up his hands as though to stop traffic. "I don't want to talk about it right now, OK? I've just got to be alone."

"Fine," Molly said with a shrug. "But what good is performing if it makes you this nervous? You're the best piano player in the school. No matter whether you make a mistake or not, nobody else in this whole auditorium can play as beautifully as you do. Remind yourself of that; think about the time you won grand prize last year and remind yourself how good you were. Your parents won't mind if you make a mistake; I know mine wouldn't."

Steve shook his head at her and closed his eyes. "I don't know why I let you get me into this."

"Now remember, I didn't force you," Molly said. He was making her uneasy. This was a different Steve from the person she knew yesterday.

He swallowed hard, held a hand to his mouth, and hurried out the exit door. Molly scrambled to her feet and followed him.

"Go away!" he commanded in a strangled voice. The campus was so silent his voice seemed to echo off the buildings. He was leaning against the wall of the auditorium with one arm, the other hand holding up his head. He gagged loudly and spat something on the ground.

"Steven." Molly's voice was gentle. "What's the matter?"

He waved a hand in her direction. "Go away! Just go inside."

"I can't leave you out here like this."

"I'll be fine. Go on in. I mean it." His eyes were hard.

"You sure?"

"Go."

Reluctantly, Molly turned and slipped quietly back inside, propping the door open with a block of wood. Steve joined her after an agonizing three minutes, sitting quietly beside her until his name was called. Molly took his cold hands in her warm ones and kissed them. "You'll do great," she whispered.

At last the program was over. Steve had performed stunningly, and the crowd had gone wild, giving him a standing ovation. He earned first prize in the serious music category. Molly and her friends had also won first prize—in the comedy category—and then, to their surprise, won the grand prize.

"I told you they'd love you," Molly said proudly as she and Steve made their way through the milling crowd to find their parents. As they inched along, strangers stopped them to offer congratulations. Molly could hardly wait to see her parents and hear how they liked the performances.

Steve led her to the very front row of the auditorium. There, a plain-looking couple were bent over a large reel-to-reel tape recorder. The man stiffened when Steve said, "Dad?" Without looking up from what he was doing, Mr. Bowker said "Hel-lo" in a singsong voice, emphasizing the first syllable.

He took his time reading his notations on the tape box, unplugging the wires and wrapping them around his arm as they waited for him to look at them. Molly studied him quietly, mildly amused at his rudeness. Not much of a first impression, she thought, amazed at how different his manners were from his son's. Steve's mother must be the one with the manners.

At last Steve's dad straightened and looked at them. Seeing Molly with Steve, he let out a snort. "Oh! Hello! Hello! And who is this young lady?" Though he smiled, his hands remained limply at his sides.

In some ways, Mr. Bowker's face reminded Molly of Santa Claus—it looked red and round and jolly. But he also had droopy cheeks and heavy bags under his eyes, and the gray ring of hair that circled the sides and back of his head looked to her like a dropped halo. His smile seemed unnatural, almost as if he had plucked it from an unseen collection.

Steve said, "Dad, I'd like you to meet Molly." Then, turning to Molly, he continued, "My dad, Lloyd Bowker."

"How do you do, Molly?" At last Lloyd stuck out a hand. His long, pasty jowls shook as he pumped her hand. "Oh, nice soft hands," he murmured appreciatively, and Molly pulled her hand away quickly. She fought a sudden urge to run, forcing herself to smile warmly and be polite instead, for these were the people who had created Steve.

"And this is my mom, Barbara."

Molly realized her expectations about the Bowkers were totally wrong. They were far from aristocratic. Barbara towered in front of her in a plain navy pantsuit, a red cardigan draped around her broad shoulders. Her black, perfectly set beauty-shop curls were sprayed into a solid cap on her head. She was quickly stuffing some knitting into a canvas bag that hung from one dimpled arm. In spite of the hair and the red rouge circles on her cheeks, she seemed warm and comfortable. Molly thought she would like getting to know her.

Mr. Bowker was rocking on his heels, sizing Molly up and down. "Your skit was . . . interesting." He emphasized the "ing," his voice rising.

"Thank you," Molly said. "It was one of the craziest parts I've ever played."

"I'm sure." Mr. Bowker's eyes were locked on her, and he chuckled insipidly. Molly chided herself for taking an instant disliking to him, but she couldn't help it. There was something about him that made her uneasy. Was it the shifty eyes or the sarcastic chuckle? Or had Leona's comments biased her? She couldn't pin it down; but whatever it was, she felt very uncomfortable. Meeting him had sucked the joy out of the evening—and yet Molly was ashamed of herself for disliking him.

They stood without saying anything for several moments while Molly scanned the crowd, looking for her parents. She started to walk away—then, remembering her manners, she said with a nod, "It was nice to meet you."

"You going?" Steve asked, and Molly nodded again.

"Not so fast, young lady," Lloyd said sardonically. "I need a picture of you two first."

"I'll be right back," she promised him.

Lloyd placed a commanding hand on her shoulder. "This will only take a minute," he said, raising his eyebrows menacingly. "Your parents can find *you* just as easily as you can find them. Steve, move over there." Lloyd pointed to a spot three feet away. Steve didn't move far enough. "Move over there—over there. Over there. Right there." His voice rose, and he spoke slower and slower, with more and more menace. He jabbed the air with a stubby finger until Steve and Molly's position satisfied him.

Molly asked, "Are you sure we should move? The flowers where we were would have made a nice backdrop." As she did so, Steve pulled her to him with a look that warned her not to say more. He squeezed her arm, forced a smile on his face, and Lloyd snapped their picture.

"*Now* you may go," Lloyd declared. Then he said, "I had you move because you were in someone else's picture, and you were in such a hurry I knew you wouldn't want to wait."

Molly felt claustrophobic around this man. She was breathing fast and shallow. She would have liked Steve better if she had never met his father. "I've got to find my folks," she said in a hurry.

"I'll go with you," Steve said.

"Oh, yes. You go along with her. We're 'just family,' " Lloyd said, forcing a cold chuckle. His words had a sarcastic ring.

Steve was obviously distressed. "We'll be right back. Can't the twins help? Or Patti?"

Lloyd puffed up his chest. "It's your program."

"I'm sorry," Steve said penitently. Molly wondered if it was always this way with his father. He turned to her weakly. "You go ahead and find your folks; I'll help here."

"OK. But don't go anywhere. They want to meet you."

At last she found her parents, and the atmosphere of care they projected felt so comforting. Brad had dressed carefully for the occasion in a brown sport coat and the olive green slacks Molly had given him for his birthday that summer. Whenever he visited Molly or her sister, he always wore something she or her sister had given him. Mom looked stunning in a new turquoise pantsuit she had bought for the occasion and had accented with a blue-and-green scarf.

Molly's parents kissed her simultaneously, one on each cheek. "You were marvelous, honey, just marvelous—as always!" her mother said. "My buttons were popping right off. And Steve! His piece was just beautiful."

"He'll enjoy hearing that," Molly said. "He was so nervous beforehand, he threw up at the back door."

"Oh, poor guy. Are his parents here?"

"Yeah. They want to meet you."

Molly wondered what Lloyd would say to her parents. With trepidation she led them back to where the Bowkers were standing and introduced them all around.

The grown-ups shook hands. Mrs. Bowker flashed her broad smile at Molly's mother.

Molly hooked her arm through Steve's. "And this is Steve."

Molly's mother said, "It's so nice to meet you. Molly's told us all about you—all good. And I loved your solo, Steve. It was just beautiful."

He said a humble, "Thank you," and Molly beamed at him. "I think he should make a record," she said.

"I think so too," her mother agreed. "Your touch was so expressive. It carried me away; I thought I was up high on the ceiling looking down." She turned to Barbara. "Your buttons must have been popping; I'll bet you were proud!"

Barbara nodded soundlessly with a giggle, her shoulders rising to meet her ears as she looked at her husband.

Mr. Bowker chuckled loudly. "Now, now. Exaggerating a little, aren't we? You weren't really on the ceiling," he said rudely, as though Molly's mother were a child. "Now I know where your daughter gets her big imagination from." He turned to Steve. "I was disappointed that you only earned first prize. You've won grand prize before. Probably because of that goof on the third measure from the end."

Steve looked sheepish. "Yeah, probably."

"I didn't hear a mistake," Molly's mother said. "It all sounded perfect to me." Her dad agreed.

Lloyd cut in with an amused smile. "Well, if you knew the piece, you'd know where he goofed. I guess we can tell who knows music and who doesn't. I have it all on tape. You can listen to it when you come home, Steve."

"Do I have to?"

"That's why I tape you. A performance isn't good enough if you don't enjoy listening to it later. If you'd practice, you might come up with some fairly decent stuff. But noooo—you don't ever have time to practice." He turned to Kate Spencer. "Thinks it's boring," he said with a snort.

Molly listened to this exchange in disbelief. She had been uneasy about meeting Steve's parents because she was concerned about them liking her. Now she didn't care how they felt about her—she didn't like *them*. Well, Steve's father, at least. Something about him made her want to run. No wonder Leona's parents were spreading rumors about the man. Unless you had been on the receiving end of his good deeds, it would be hard to appreciate him.

At last Molly's dad said he had some things in the car for Molly. She and her parents said good night and excused themselves. Molly pressed a hand to Steve's arm and told him goodbye. In his eyes, she saw the haunted look of a caged animal. She hated leaving Steve with those people. What kind of parents were they, anyway? What permanent marks might they have made on Steve? Was it possible he would go through some sort of metamorphosis as he got older and become like his father? Had she seen just a tiny glimpse of that this evening? A nagging uneasiness told her she was entering dangerous waters. But she loved being with Steve. Was the behavior of the father reason enough to break up with him?

CHAPTER

3

December 1967

To Molly, it would remain a December day like no other. The clean, crisp air was scented with pine. As the sun warmed the park benches scattered across the campus, a thin cloak of white vapor rose from each. With Christmas vacation beginning the next day, Molly and Steve took a few moments between classes to relax together in the fresh air.

The bench creaked as they lowered themselves onto it. Steve slipped his right arm around Molly's shoulder, attempting to pull her head under his chin despite their bulky coats. With his other hand, he pulled his ankle up onto his knee, smiling like a man content with the world.

"I'm going to miss you really badly starting tomorrow," he murmured, rubbing his cheek against Molly's silky hair.

"I'll miss you too. But Christmas break will go fast," she said toward his steady heartbeat.

"Maybe."

"Perhaps you could drive up to Idaho for a visit."

"No, my dad would never allow that."

"Then maybe I could visit you," she said, trying another angle.

"No, I don't think so."

"Why not?"

"Well, your parents wouldn't want you driving in this weather—it's two days from my house to yours."

"We could all come. Dad could drive," Molly said.

"I don't know. I mean, it's not that I don't want to see you over vacation," Steve said, trying to explain. "But my dad's different from your dad. Our folks wouldn't have much in common; I'm afraid your folks would be bored."

"But I've never visited at your house, and we've been seeing each other for nearly three months now. And I'd like to see Crescent City and the ocean."

"Someday I'll show you," he promised, knowing it couldn't be until after they were married. The discomfort Molly showed upon meeting his dad had scared him. He feared that if she and her parents spent any extended time with his family, she would go the way of all his other girlfriends. She was such a special creature, he knew he couldn't lose her.

"It isn't that I don't want you to come," he said. "I've got lots to show you at my house and at my grandparents' place. There's a redwood tree my Grandpa Feldman planted when I was just a little guy. I could jump over it easily then."

"I'm sure you were cute! Who's Grandpa Feldman?"

"He's my mother's dad. He's cool; you'll like him."

"Where does he live?"

"He and Grandma live in Astoria, Oregon. Grandpa used to be a logger, but he's a farmer now; always has loved trees and other growing things. He planted a tree at his house when each of his kids were born and for any other occasion he decided was special. Mom's tree is a cherry tree."

"Do your other grandparents live nearby too?"

"No, they're down in Los Angeles. We don't see them much. They're kind of stuffy. We call them 'Grandmother' and 'Grandfather.'"

"Just like Heidi."

"Heidi who?"

"You know, the book *Heidi*—about the little girl and her alm-uncle . . . she called him 'Grandfather.'" She laughed deliciously, as she always did with Steve—a bubbly laugh that seemed to come from her toes and refreshed her.

Then she shivered inside her coat, and Steve said, "You're cold. We'd better go in."

"I'll be OK for a while."

They talked a while longer and then sat in companionable silence for a few minutes before they ambled toward the dormitory with their fingers entwined. When they reached the steps, Steve led Molly to a private spot every couple knew about behind the towering holly bushes. There, he turned Molly to face him and pulled her to him, wrapping his arms gently around her shoulders. "You are the happiest person I've ever known," he murmured, laying his cheek gently on the top of her fragrant hair.

"You make me happy," she said. Through his jacket, she could hear, again, the strong beating of his heart.

"I love you. I want to make you happy forever," Steve said softly. His blue-green eyes were serious, yet gentle. He turned her face to his. "Marry me, Molly Spencer."

"It's quite soon," Molly said cautiously. "I hardly know your family."

"Maybe it's better that way. When we're married, we can do things our own way—have a house of our own and plant our own trees."

Molly's heart was leaping so hard she found it difficult to breathe. Steve was wonderful. But should they know each other better before they married? Would it make a difference?

"I'm scared," she whispered. Steve brushed the back of his hand gently across the smooth line of her jaw as though it were fine china. Molly managed to say, "But I promise to think about it . . . I love you too, Steve."

He smiled. "Kiss me quick before I die."

"Are you dying?"

"I will if you don't kiss me."

"That sounds like a line from a cheap novel," Molly said wryly. But she slipped her arms up around his shoulders. He lifted her chin with his fingertips and kissed her. It was a rose-petal kiss, soft and gentle—yet the intense look in his eyes shot a thrill through her. Being in his arms felt so right. But the seriousness of what Steve was asking her made her shiver.

It seemed Molly couldn't get the Bowker family off her mind during Christmas vacation. She kept remembering Mr. Bowker's odd comments and mysterious control over Steve. He seemed, in fact, to dominate all the family members. She had met

Steve's brothers and sister during a weekend visit they made to the college in November. Molly thought it strange that Mr. Bowker was still tickling his daughter, Patti, under the arms, even though she was sixteen. But she seemed to enjoy being tickled to the floor and didn't ask him to stop.

At home, Molly soon discovered that her parents had some reservations about the Bowkers. She had always taken the side of the underdog, so she rather naturally fell into defending Steve's family whenever her parents made unfavorable comparisons between them and her sister's future in-laws. Anyway, she was sure that once she was a Bowker she would be able to change things.

Steve seemed so confident, yet he seemed to need her desperately. She found his need both gratifying and frightening. Molly was uncertain what Steve would do if she broke up with him; he wasn't strong enough in the face of trouble. To spare Steve immense pain, she decided that she would make a life with him that would fulfill her dreams for the future. She would tell Steve she would marry him. She would rescue him. She would make it work; it would be her mission.

Steve and Molly were married in August of 1968 in a large and joyful ceremony at her home church in Idaho. Her father gave a special wedding blessing. Knowing how much Lloyd enjoyed performing, Molly had him sing a solo. She also found a place in the wedding party for each of Steve's siblings.

The Bowkers warmly welcomed Molly into their family. "You're just the kind of granddaughter-in-law I would have picked for Steve," Grandma Feldman exclaimed in Kate Spencer's presence, and Kate smiled quietly.

After the honeymoon, Steve and Molly returned to Crescent City and moved into an apartment that overlooked the ocean. Molly knew her mother was concerned about their dropping out of college, but was trying not to interfere. Steve resumed his apprenticeship with Lloyd's landscaping company, and Molly found work as a secretary. She promised her mother they would return to college someday.

CHAPTER

4

September 1969

Grandma and Grandpa Feldman lived in a ninety-year-old house on the side of a heavily wooded hill that looked out over the ocean. A network of well-used trails wound through the woods, pathways made by generations of deer, skunks, raccoons, and toddling children. The Feldmans, Grace and Stu, had moved to this house in the shadow of the Astoria Tower as newlyweds in 1922. Barbara had been born the following year, when Grace was seventeen. Three more children followed during the next fifteen years, two of them girls: Aunt Vera and Aunt Louise—the youngest in the family. The only son had died of a brain tumor at the age of ten.

A little over a year after their wedding, Steve and Molly came for a visit. The house's cut-glass windows sparkled like diamonds as Steve started up the winding drive. They passed the apple orchard, heavy with fruit, and the bing cherry tree that Barbara had planted when she was just ten. Every summer Steve had picked the cherries from that tree and sold them to the faithful neighbors, keeping the profits.

An enormous vegetable garden came into view on the left, on the only flat piece of land around—a plot that Grandpa had carved out of the mountain. He was out there between the tomato plants with his rototiller, turning the fine, brown earth. The smell of the rich soil floated in through the window, and Molly inhaled it deeply. It was Grandpa's garden that had brought them here this time. Grandpa had done some canning and had offered them some if they would come and pick it up.

33

But it wasn't the food alone that brought them here. Molly loved visiting Grandpa and Grandma Feldman. Even short visits with them left her feeling refreshed and ready to take on the challenges of life.

The car's engine had not even stopped when the back screen door swung open with its characteristic squeak and Grandma Feldman hurried out with her cane, a broad smile on her face. She stood beside the back porch with her arms wide open. "Oh, you're here! Hi, honey."

Molly hurried to hug her. "How've you been? I saw Grandpa out in the garden."

"Oh, yes. He said if he didn't get the tomatoes weeded before you got here, Steve would spend all his time out in the garden instead of visiting."

Molly chuckled. "He might anyway. I noticed the cherry tree's been picked."

"Yes, one of the neighbor boys picked it for us in June. We couldn't sell the cherries; Stu didn't spray them this year, and the bugs got to them." Grandma held out her arms to Steve and beckoned to him. "Come on, honey, you too."

"Hi, Grandma. How're you doing? I see you're using the cane again." He towered above her.

"Yes, my old arthritis is acting up again. But as long as I stay inside, I do OK. I have lots to do now, with that baby of yours coming on. You didn't give me much time to finish your wedding afghan before you made me start on the baby's."

"We've been married a year, Grandma," Steve reminded her.

Laughing, they moved inside while Steve added, "It was a year in August, so it's been more than a year; it's been thirteen months, in fact."

"I guess so. Time flies when you're getting old, you know."

The house was small and cozy. Its kitchen was everyone's favorite room; it had a nook that jutted out over the hillside and gave a commanding view of the ocean. The nook's built-in, cafe-type table was comfortably cluttered with an ancient toaster and a wooden napkin holder that Steve had made when he took wood-working as a boy. When they ate, they could watch the hypnotic motion of the creaming surf against the tawny sand. And way out on the horizon, the heaving, turquoise swells were mesmerizing as they cast glittering sea pennies toward the light-blue sky.

The living room extended the kitchen, great room style, and was furnished with a worn davenport and two equally worn rocking chairs facing the TV. *National Geographic*s spanning several decades crowded the brick fireplace. Grandma had explained once that she and Grandpa were worried that the chimney was so old, it might burn them up in their sleep, so they never lighted a fire. Instead, when they wanted to warm their feet, they used electric heaters.

Grandma shuffled to her rocking chair and gestured toward the couch. "Have a seat, make yourselves comfortable—if you're not too tired of sitting. Oh, and Steve, honey, would you mind calling Vera and letting her know you're here? She wanted to come over and see you the minute you arrived."

Steve agreed cheerfully and went to the phone as Grandma picked up the beautiful, pastel green blanket she was crocheting. Raising her eyebrows, she addressed Molly. "Now, tell me again—when is the baby due? In May sometime?"

"May 31," Molly said. "Seven-and-a-half months to go."

"Have you been awfully sick?"

"Not too bad, really. I'm almost looking forward to getting sick so it seems like it's really happening. I still can't believe it."

"Enjoy it while you can," Grandma admonished.

After Steve called Aunt Vera, he returned to the couch, picked up a magazine, and started idly leafing through it. "Well, there's one excited auntie. She didn't want to talk. Said she'd talk in person."

"Is she on her way over, then?" Grandma asked.

"Yeah. Said she'd be here in five minutes."

"She will too," Grandma said, chuckling. "My, we're all so excited about the baby—our first one."

Molly smiled happily. Barbara's family was so warm and comfortable, it hardly seemed possible she had known them for only a little over two years. Sometimes she wondered if they were just trying to make her feel comfortable, if they really loved her as much as they said they did. Feeling self-conscious, she said,

"If you think you're excited now, just wait till Patti has a baby."

"It will be some time. She has to get married first," Grandma said. "But when her baby comes, it will be no more special than yours, and it may not receive even as much attention, because yours is the first. And everyone loves you, Molly."

Grandpa came clomping in from outside and placed a bucket of fresh tomatoes on the table. "Tomato sandwiches and corn on the cob for supper tonight."

"And some of your famous cucumber-and-sour-cream salad?" Molly asked eagerly.

Grandpa winked at her. "If that's what you crave," he promised, "then that's what you'll get."

"I've been thinking about it all the way here."

"Then it's settled. Cucumber salad as well." The room fell silent, and Grandpa seemed to realize he had cut in on their conversation. "Well, go on, keep talking. Don't let me interrupt. I'll just start peeling the cukes."

"We were just talking about Patti. You heard she's engaged," Steve said.

"Yes, I did. But she's a bit young, I think."

Grandma cut in with a chuckle. "Don't get him started on that."

Grandpa smiled broadly. "I'll reserve my comments till later," he said, and Grandma smiled indulgently, obviously still enamored with his diplomatic ways. She turned to Steve, her fingers working away on the blanket as if they had a mind of their own. "And how have you been enjoying working for your father, Steve?"

He shrugged. "Oh, it's OK. I wouldn't want to be a landscaper for the rest of my life, though. Actually," he glanced quickly at Molly as though to get her approval, "I've been thinking of becoming a doctor."

"A doctor! That's a long road to haul."

"I know. But it fascinates me."

Grandma nodded. "It's a very noble profession. And if you want to do it, you can; you've got the brains, honey. But it will be difficult with the baby."

"I know. But, as Molly says, others have done it. Why not me?"

"You been saving your money?"

"I wish. Dad's not been able to pay me regularly because his customers don't give him a steady cash flow. But they bought us a used washer and dryer and the old car, so I guess that counts for something."

The pay situation was a sore point with Molly. For the past year they had been living on her income as a secretary, and there had been nothing to put aside for savings. The appliances had cost $25 apiece; the car, $300. The way she figured it, at $7 an hour, Steve should have been making $56 a day, $280 a week. But all they had to show for all Steve's work were two old appliances, an eight-year-old car, and an occasional partial paycheck.

Grandma was of the same opinion as Molly. "Seems like you should have gotten more out of the deal than you did."

"Well, I am now. I'm taking a few courses at the community college, and Dad's paying for them."

"I see." Grandma's lips tightened as if she were trying to repress some comments. For a few minutes they sat in silence as her fingers crocheted in tiny movements like miniature pistons.

Steve picked up a fringed throw pillow and hugged it, scooting down to place his head on the back of the couch. So many memories this place evoked—most of them happy. For some reason, being at Grandma and Grandpa Feldmans' diluted his dad's dominance. As a boy, Steve had stayed by Grandpa's side whenever they visited, as far away from his father as he could get. When he was with Grandpa, he learned to like himself a little. Grandpa always pointed out what Steve could do right; in contrast, his dad pointed out his faults. When Grandpa entered the house, he came in whistling, bringing sunshine; Dad plodded in like an electric storm, bringing gloom and darkness. It was strange how different the atmosphere could be around different people.

Molly sat fascinated with Grandma's crocheting for several minutes. Then she said, "I'm making a family tree for the baby. Would this be a good time for you to tell me about Steve's side?"

"Sure, honey. What do you need to know?"

"Well, your maiden name and when you were born and something about what your dad did and stuff."

Grandma's mind was sharp; she recalled names, dates, and events as though they had happened yesterday. The family had a rich history of logging and fishing up and down the coast, as well as heart-wrenching losses like Uncle Brian's death from a brain tumor and Great Aunt Midge's daughter, who died of appendicitis at the age of six.

"Do you know anything about the Bowker side?" Molly asked.

Grandma Feldman thought for a moment. "I guess I don't, honey. You know that Lloyd was an only child. I think his dad had a sister, but I don't know much else about them."

"That's OK. I'll ask Grandmother about it when I see her. I only met her once—at the wedding—and we didn't have much time to talk."

"Yes, she would probably know."

The crunching sound of tires on gravel drifted in from outdoors, accompanied by the incessant honking of a horn.

"Vera's here," Grandpa said. He threw open the windows and waved a leathery arm—all the while mumbling good-naturedly, "We hear you, we hear you."

Molly chuckled as Grandpa explained with a shake of the head, "She always comes in like that when she's excited. She still has the energy of a teenager, and she's pretty near fifty!"

Steve hurried outside to greet Aunt Vera. She came in like a whirlwind, loaded with grocery bags filled with "treats" she had bought on her way. "Howdy, howdy!" A tight hug for Molly and a pat on the belly. "How's our baby?"

"Fine, I guess."

"Good, good. And why isn't the table set, Dad? I brought a roast I just took out of the oven, and it's going to get cold if you don't hurry with your part."

"We can keep it warm in the oven. The kettle's on the stove for the corn. You just go on into the other room and visit with Molly and Steve. I'll get everything fixed out here."

"All right, then. Take a lesson, Molly. Never ask Grandpa twice about helping in the kitchen. If he says go, then go—or he might change his mind." A loud cackle escaped Vera's lips, and no one could resist chuckling along.

An hour later, after they had enjoyed the buttery corn, crisp vegetables, and roast, and everyone had pushed away from the table, Vera said, "Well, we heard Patti's getting married."

"Yeah. Did she call you?"

"Yes, she called Mother last week."

Grandma said, "And that's why I have so much to do. After I finish your baby's afghan, it'll be time to start on the one for Patti's wedding. And then she'll probably have a baby right away too. You should have spaced these events out a little more."

"Patti's only eighteen, isn't she?" Vera observed.

"That's mighty young," Grandma said.

"She'll be nineteen by the time she gets married. That's how old we were," Steve said. "And you were sixteen, Grandma, so you don't have much room to talk."

Molly was surprised by Steve's brashness, which resembled Lloyd's. Rather direct remarks like this had been coming with increasing frequency since the wedding, and also attempts, many of them successful, to manipulate her—as Lloyd did Barbara. But it was Steve's brooding silences that bothered her most; she always wondered what he was brooding about.

"Steve," she said now, trying to smooth over his comments, "that's not very polite."

Steve chuckled. "I'm sorry, but you know what I mean, don't you, Grandma?"

"Of course, honey." She reached out and placed a warm hand on his arm. "I understand why you and your sister wanted to get married so young."

"Well, wouldn't you, with a father like that?" Vera burst out. Then she slapped her lips. "Sorry. Sorry. I didn't say that. But you know what I mean, Steve. I know he hasn't been easy to live with. When you were just a little guy, about three, you asked to live with us."

"I did?"

"Uh-huh. Your family was visiting, and you came to me and said, 'I don't want to go home with Daddy. I want to live with Auntie.' I think maybe you had gotten into trouble and they had spanked you or something. I said, 'Well, your mommy and daddy love you, and they would miss you if you lived with me.' But you were serious and said, 'No, I want to live with Auntie.' I think you liked the country.It was so cute."

Steve smiled wanly. A grain of salt on the table caught his attention, and he rolled it around under his fingertip as though deep in thought.

Grandpa asked in his forthright way, "What do your parents think of Patti's marriage, Steve?"

Steve's attention did not leave the grain of salt under his finger. "Oh, Dad had a fit at first and kind of sulked around the house and at work. It was pretty uncomfortable. But now he seems to have changed and says he's looking forward to lots of grandchildren. It's like he has a new lease on life—he almost seems more excited about the marriage than Patti is."

Steve went on. "I know we're looking forward to *our* little one. He might be here by the time Patti gets married. Then we can show him off to everyone—even steal the show, maybe."

Everyone chuckled at the thought of upstaging Patti, knowing it would never happen. Patti was Lloyd's favorite; he would make sure the spotlight was always on her.

Molly said, "This seems to be the year for babies. My sister's having one in March. Her husband just got a job teaching at the church school in Crescent City, so I'm going to be able to see it right away and learn a few things before my own comes. Hers will be the first one for my family."

"Lloyd's birthday is in March—March 10," Grandma said.

Steve was surprised. "I didn't know that."

"I did," Molly said. "He's hoping it comes on his birthday."

They all enjoyed a good hour of visiting before cleaning up the kitchen. Then they played Scrabble under the yellow light over the table, sipping hot chocolate between turns.

By the time they had played a couple games, everyone was yawning so grandly that they decided to turn out the lights and call it a day. Molly and Steve crept up the creaky stairs to the attic bedroom where his mother had slept as a child. There was so much history here. Scrapbooks and two more decades of *National Geographic*s lined up in order on a shelf that had a neat flowered skirt. They knew so much about Steve's mother's side, so little about his father's. The Bowkers seemed to have no past, as though they had dropped out of the sky.

CHAPTER

5

1970

It was a brilliant morning in March. Molly studied her changing profile in the full-length mirror across from her bed and patted her tummy protectively. The baby seemed to be growing nicely. She smiled, feeling domesticated and fulfilled. All her dreams were coming true.

She and Steve had moved from their apartment to a small house that also stood on a hill overlooking the ocean. The house was old and nothing fancy: two bedrooms, cracked linoleum in the kitchen, rust in the sinks, moss on the roof. But it was a house, not an apartment. To freshen it, Molly had hung organza curtains that bellied out in the wind, and she had hidden the holes in the linoleum with scatter rugs. The tulips she had planted in November added brilliant splashes of red under the front window; they were tall enough to join the startling blue sea in the scene she saw through that window whenever she sat down in their newly purchased rocking chair.

Molly's eyes took in her bedroom's decor lovingly. An antique dressing table with a central mirror and two hinged side mirrors sat against the wall opposite the bed, lacy doilies and multi-faceted crystal perfume bottles of various shapes and colors adorning it. A round, low maple stool with a cushioned tapestry seat squatted in front of the full-length mirror. The table and stool had belonged to her grandmother. Above the bed's brass headboard were two framed sprays of wildflowers that Molly had picked and pressed on her honeymoon nearly two years before. Framed reprints of paintings of flower gardens in greens and pinks and yellows hung on the wall across from the door, part of a collage that also included gold-framed photos of family members, Molly and Steve's wedding certificate, and quilting squares that Molly had made herself—to match the colors of the flowers. A white eyelet spread covered the bed, and Molly had brightened it with throw pillows in soft green and pink and yellow.

When the sun shone in, as it did this morning, the room's warmth and color called for someone to stay all day—but Molly had to get to work. With a sigh she pulled on a navy blue maternity pantsuit with a white sailor collar and slipped her feet into navy blue walking shoes. Sitting at her typewriter for long periods of time was becoming difficult, and the baby kicked and squirmed each time the phone rang. But in just one month, she would quit work and begin to get the house ready for the baby's arrival.

The drive to the office took just ten minutes. When she arrived and tore off yesterday's calendar page, she realized that today was March 10 and Barbara was planning a birthday party for Lloyd that evening. Molly dreaded going. Now that she was one of the family—and pregnant—Lloyd's comments had become particularly personal. He patted her protuberant belly much too often for her comfort and just laughed when she asked him not to do so. She would have preferred that Barbara and Lloyd go out to celebrate his birthday privately, but Barbara wanted the whole family there. Steve seemed to think it was important to be there too.

The day passed much too rapidly. At about four o'clock, as Molly was running the day's letters through the postage meter, she received a phone call she had been waiting for.

"Molly?"

"Yes?"

"Hi! This is Linda. I'm at the hospital."

"You are? Have you had the baby?"

"About half an hour ago. It's a girl!"

"Oh, Linda! Congratulations! I'm coming right over from work. This is Lloyd's birthday, too, but I'll skip the party. When are visiting hours?"

"Not until seven. Seven to eight. And they don't make any allowances, so you have to be here on time."

"I will be. Oh—what did you name her?"

"We haven't decided yet, but we're thinking of Brittany. Kevin suggested it."

"That's cute. Brittany Ashton. Oh, I can't wait to see her. Does she look like you?"

"We don't know whom she looks like. Maybe you can tell."

"Oh, I am absolutely thrilled! Let me finish up here, and I'll see you soon! Goodbye." Molly hung up the phone carefully, deep in thought. She had to call Steve and let him know about the baby. Visiting hours would cut into the party. Barbara would need to know they couldn't come; she would understand.

Molly dialed the shop number quickly, and Lloyd answered. "Hi. Is Steve there?" She had never been able to call Lloyd "Dad." To get around it, she tried to catch his eye and launch directly into her question or comment. On the phone she also went right to business.

The phone clunked to the desk. Molly could picture the scene easily in her mind. It was a small room just big enough for the desk and the squeaky green chair with the torn upholstery that Lloyd spent most of the day in, now that Steve was there to supervise the workers. The desk was old; yellowed pine with a brown leather top crowded full of assorted stacks of papers and plant catalogs, wire spindles, frayed phone books, and a shiny black phone. It was covered with statues the kids had given him many years before that proclaimed variations of the theme "World's Greatest Dad." Similar plaques adorned the wall—but remarkably, there were no pictures of the children who had given him these honors. That oddity had been the first thing that struck Molly when she had seen it. It seemed that Lloyd put great stock in looking like a great father. The fact that he was a dictator was a well-kept secret.

Molly heard Steve's voice and the clomp of his boots as he approached the desk.

"Hello?"

"Hi, Steve. It's Molly. Guess what! Linda's had her baby!"

"Today?"

"About half an hour ago. It's a girl, and they're thinking of naming her Brittany. They want us to come to the hospital tonight."

"But it's Dad's party."

"Oh, I know. But he'll understand, won't he?"

"Maybe we could go afterwards," Steve suggested.

"Visiting hours are just during the party—from seven to eight. If we don't go then, we can't see them." She heard Steve and Lloyd discussing something faintly before Steve came back on the phone.

"Why can't we just wait and see the baby once Linda gets home? Dad said he'll go with us. He and Mom have an oak rocking chair for Linda that they refinished and a blanket and sweater Mom's crocheted. They want us to be there when they give it to them."

Molly couldn't understand Steve's reluctance. "Steve," she said firmly. "You don't seem to catch the importance of what has just happened. My only sister has just had a baby, and I can't wait to see it. It seems like an eternity till visiting hours get here. I can come again with your folks after Linda gets home, but I want you to come with me tonight. Please? Your dad's got Patti and the twins and his wife to celebrate with him; they won't miss us. This is important."

"Molly." Steve sounded agonized. "Don't make this any more difficult on me than it already is."

"I don't see any difficulty making the choice. Can't you just tell your dad you're not coming?"

"No, Molly. I can't."

"Why not?"

Steve made an impatient sound. "Look. We'll talk when I get home after work."

"I won't *be* home. When I get out of here in an hour, I have to stop by the post office and then go shopping for the baby. There's a Sears store out by the hospital, and a McDonald's, so I'll just catch a bite to eat there and see Linda at seven. I wish you could come too. Tell your mom I'm sorry, but I'm sure she can understand why I can't make it."

"OK. 'Bye. I love you."

"Love you too. G'bye."

Molly returned home at eight-thirty that night feeling exuberant. "Oh, Steve, the baby's so beautiful. Looks just like Linda, I think. I had a great time. How was your evening?"

"Awful. Dad spent the whole evening making snide comments about how the baby didn't know you were there and wouldn't have missed you—rubbing it in. I don't think Mom understood why you stood them up, either."

"I can't believe it. Steve, this is the first baby in the family. It's so exciting. Your mom could have postponed the party till tomorrow night if my being there were so important. I can't understand it." She turned her back to him to stare out of the window at the moonlight glimmering on the water for a few moments, her hands cradling her belly. "Just wait till our baby comes—then they'll know how it feels!"

Steve stood behind her and put his arms around her shoulders in a protective gesture. "Calm down now. It's not good for the baby when you're upset. Ours is a lucky baby to have a mother like you. And it will be the most beautiful baby ever."

"I don't know," Molly warned him. "The competition's pretty stiff!" She turned to Steve, a smile illuminating her face. "Brittany's awfully cute, Steve. You should have seen her."

"I will. Soon."

Two days later, when Linda left the hospital, Molly and Steve were waiting at her home. They had hung balloons and crepe paper by the front door and over the dining table and had a warm meal waiting for her and her husband Kevin.

Linda moved slowly from the car to the house and shuffled into the living room while Kevin followed with the tiny pink blanket. Against the green carpet and furnishings, Linda's skin was pale. "You look wasted," Molly said gently. "Here. Sit in the chair of honor." She pulled out the upholstered chair at the head of the table. Kevin padded down the hall to place the baby in her crib. "Dinner will be served shortly. Are you hungry?" Molly asked.

"Famished. All I've wanted to do since Brittany was born is eat and sleep."

"When's Mom coming?"

"Tomorrow, I think. But she can't stay long because of their move."

"Your folks are moving?" Steve asked.

"Oh, yes. Didn't I tell you?" Molly took a salad bowl out of the refrigerator and pressed it into Steve's hands. "Can you put this on?

"Dad's been promoted. He's going to teach religion at the university in Michigan."

"Michigan!" It was the last place Steve would have expected.

"Yeah. Mom's not too happy, but their income is going to increase, and Daddy's promised her she can fly out when our baby comes, and we can fly back there for visits and stuff. I don't know how I missed telling you. I told your mom, and she promised to spread herself thin between Linda's baby and mine."

Linda smiled weakly. "She's so sweet. I'm sure she'll make a good grandma. And Lloyd's really good with children too. Brittany won't know he and Barbara aren't her real grandparents. Are your folks pretty excited about your baby, Steve?"

"Yeah, I guess so. But mostly they're working on Patti's wedding."

"And when is that?" Linda asked.

"The middle of June—the fifteenth, or something like that."

Molly placed the last dish, a bubbling casserole of lasagna, on the table and unwrapped the steaming garlic bread before sitting down. "I'm afraid I insulted Lloyd by coming to see Brittany the other night instead of going to his birthday party."

"Barbara called yesterday and told me they share the same birthday," Linda said. "What a coincidence! They're bringing a surprise of some sort over tomorrow. Can you come again?"

"No problem!" Molly replied.

Steve had his napkin in his lap. "Well, I hate to interrupt, but I'm starving. Let's have the blessing and get on with the meal and talk about something besides my father."

Linda and Kevin looked at Steve quizzically before bowing their heads for prayer. But, as Steve had requested, nothing more was said of Lloyd throughout the meal.

CHAPTER

6

June 15, 1970

The day of Patti's wedding could not have been more perfect. The temperature was in the low seventies—unexpectedly cool for the middle of June—and the sun, blinking through the scattered clouds that drifted by overhead, offered bursts of warmth and color throughout the day. Molly hoped it would stay that way till the wedding started that evening.

Teddy, just seven days old, kept Molly quite busy, demanding to be fed every two hours. Though Aunt Vera had said she and the other aunties could do most of the preparations for Patti's wedding themselves, Molly had made a point of staying at her in-laws' house all day, helping out as much as she could. Vera had taken ample opportunity to put her feet up by offering to rock Teddy to sleep whenever he cried.

There wasn't much privacy or quiet space in the house. It was a typical "sixties" house; a brown box like all the others down the street. A clump of white birch trees huddled together in one corner of the yard, and Barbara's patient tending of the petunias planted in the brick flower boxes along the front windows had yielded an abundance of blooms.

The overhanging roof sheltered the living room from direct sun, making it a rather dark and cold room. The gold shag rug blended nicely with the mustard-yellow couch that sat under the front window. There was an old upright piano on one wall and a gold wing-backed chair that was reserved for Grandmother Bowker whenever she visited because it was easiest for her to get in and out of. Other, plumper chairs were scattered around the room, all of them facing a stocky coffee table that bore plastic orange flowers in a traditional arrangement.

Grandma Feldman had mentioned to Molly that Barbara and Lloyd's twenty-fifth wedding anniversary was in just a few days, and Molly had asked Patti if she minded sharing the reception with them. It amazed Molly that not one of the Bowkers' own children knew when their parents' anniversary was. It was certainly a big surprise to Patti.

Since Patti was the only daughter, Molly thought she would want to plan something for her parents herself. "A twenty-fifth wedding anniversary is a landmark," Molly had said. "We've got to do something!" But Patti was preoccupied with her own wedding, and she was happy to let Molly plan something instead.

That morning, during a brief intermission between sessions of nursing her baby, Molly had slipped downtown and bought a silver-plated serving tray. She had had a family tree engraved on it that included Lloyd's and Barbara's names and the names of their children, her own name, and Roger, Patti's husband-to-be, and little Teddy, the first grandchild. She asked Steve to prepare a short speech to give just before they presented the tray to his parents at the reception, but he said he preferred not to. Patti also declined, and since the twins were too young to make speeches, Molly prepared a little talk honoring them for reaching twenty-five years. Putting up with Lloyd for that long must have tested Barbara's endurance, and she deserved some recognition for it.

By lunchtime, Molly was back at the Bowkers', exhausted. She really wanted to go home. But, knowing that Aunt Vera and Grandma Feldman loved holding Teddy, she stayed into the afternoon. Staying at the Bowkers' added another strain—it meant being around Lloyd, and by now, she could barely stand to be in the same room with him.

Lloyd exacerbated the situation by frequently forcing himself into Molly's space. For the third time that day, he had unnecessarily plodded into the living room while she was nursing Teddy and settled across from her on the couch, leaning back against the cushions with narrowed eyes. He held an unopened magazine in his hand, apparently as some sort of "cover" if

Barbara should ask what he was doing in there.

All the rest of the multitudinous relatives had found something to do; why not Lloyd? Molly could think of a thousand things he should be doing as father of the bride. Couldn't he see that as the mother of a newborn, Molly was so exhausted she didn't care to visit? She wasn't good at this business of nursing a baby yet, either. And while she tried to keep a receiving blanket laid over her chest for modesty, having to cover up made the job that much harder. Everyone else left her some privacy when they saw what she was doing, everyone but Lloyd.

For some reason, Lloyd had been behaving suggestively since she had arrived that morning. Fully dressed initially, he had taken a shower midmorning after washing the car. Molly had been surprised to meet him walking down the hall to the bathroom that was closest to the kitchen, clad in nothing but a small towel that he held loosely around his loins. He had raised his eyebrows and grinned at her as she passed.

When Molly asked why he didn't use the bathroom near his bedroom, since there were so many visitors milling around, he said something inane about that being Barbara's bathroom and he "just wasn't used to taking a shower there." As he answered, his eyes had gleamed in a dark and lurid way as though to suggest that she was privy to something intimate.

On his return from the shower, again clad only in the skimpy towel, he had made a point of stopping in the kitchen to ask Barbara what she was making for lunch.

When Molly had suggested that he wear a robe, he had slouched to his bedroom and lay on his bed staring at the ceiling, talking to no one for about an hour. Barbara had giggled and tried to explain that he was "just nervous about giving his daughter up to another man," and assured everyone that he would be back to his old self once they left for the wedding that evening. He had a solo to sing, after all, and he loved to perform.

Having recovered from his hurt feelings of that morning, here he was again, following Molly like a malevolent shadow. Molly caught his eye. "I'm sorry," she said gently, "I'm not very good at this yet, and I need a little privacy. Do you mind?"

Lloyd made a sound like "hrmph" and laid the magazine

down beside him. "Oh. I'm sorry. I didn't know. I thought you would feed him in your room if you wanted to be alone," he said scornfully.

"Well, it's Patti's room, and she's packing up her things in there. I can't go anywhere else," Molly told him. She didn't know why, but her skin was crawling like it had when she was eight and a man on the street had fondled her chest as he passed. Leona's words of years ago and her own intuitions were making her extremely uncomfortable. She hoped there was nothing to them. But she had noticed that her intuitions didn't often mislead her.

Barbara's cheery little voice called from the kitchen. She had antennae that seemed to sense when Lloyd was disturbing someone, and rather than put him in his place, she always called him to some job she needed doing—only if he wanted to, of course. "Lloyd, if you have time, dear, I need your help."

"Oh. Sure, dear. Molly just kicked me out of my own living room." He made an attempt at chuckling, but there was an edge to his remark.

Barbara responded with the forced laugh she used whenever she suspected Lloyd's feelings had been hurt. Waving her hands in the air as though to clear away the mood, she said, "Oh, well, Molly will be done soon. Do you mind taking the gifts to the car? You're so good at packing things in. If you'll take a load of gifts now, we'll have plenty of room for everyone when we leave for the church after supper."

"My, aren't we organized?" Lloyd said sarcastically. He loaded his arms with gifts. As he turned toward the door to the garage, Barbara put up a hand to stabilize the load. Lloyd jumped on her immediately. "Would you stop that!" he demanded. "I don't drop things like you do."

"OK, OK," Barbara tittered. "I'll just let you take care of that, then, and I won't worry about you."

"Thank you," Lloyd said scornfully—as though he had just been rendered a favor.

With him out of the room, Molly allowed herself to lean back in the chair and close her eyes. Feeling warm and cozy with the sweet-smelling baby in her arms, she dozed off. Suddenly, she awoke to the sound of a newspaper crackling. It was Lloyd on the sofa again.

"I'm sorry," he said, grinning, "you and the baby looked so cute sleeping there together, I was hoping you'd wake up so I could tell you." It was unusual of him to want to share his personal feelings.

The baby was finished nursing, so Molly put herself together underneath the blanket and leaned her head back against the cushion again. She didn't feel like talking. Her mind was racing, feverishly calculating the best way to leave without being rude. Although she didn't feel safe alone with him, she felt she must be polite because he was, after all, her father-in-law.

"It's incredible," Lloyd said dreamily.

"What?" Molly said, not opening her eyes.

"What your body has done. First, you make a baby, and then you make food for it."

Molly nodded heavily.

"Men these days are so lucky. They get to see their babies being born. I've always wondered—what does it feel like to have something that big coming out between your legs?"

Startled, Molly jerked her head up and opened her eyes. Lloyd was leaning forward, staring at her intently. His eyes were cold as marbles. Molly said, "I can't believe you said that." She glared at him and shuddered ever so slightly before turning her head to avoid the indecency in his gaze. She looked around her, hoping someone would come into the room and interrupt this conversation—but the house was strangely silent. "Where is everyone?" She spoke toward the hall; she couldn't bring herself to look at him.

"They went to the church with the gifts," he said evenly. There was a note of expectation in his voice, and Molly was afraid he might see this as an opportunity.

"I thought *you* were going to do that," she said.

"I got busy."

"Did Steve go too?"

"I don't know *where* Steve is," Lloyd told her mysteriously. He was grinning sardonically. "We tried to give you some privacy, like you wanted." He paused and then asked, "What does it feel like to have something sucking on your nipples like that?"

Molly swallowed hard and gathered up the baby. It was all so sad, her child's having this—this strange man as a grandfather. She couldn't understand what made him the kind of person he was.

Molly's hands felt weak, and she realized she was shaking. She looked toward the kitchen again, but no one was there. A fog had rolled in while she had napped, and with all the lights off, it had become dark in the house. Fighting for self-control, she heard herself mumble, "Those are awfully personal questions you're asking."

Then, standing up quickly, she clutched Teddy to her chest protectively and hurried down the hall to Patti's room. Her legs felt as unsteady as a toddler's, and the hall seemed to go on forever. Pushing into the room and closing the door, she fumbled for the lock. A low moan escaped her lips when she discovered that there was none—Lloyd could come in after her if he wanted to.

The baby raised his tiny fists and stretched, his mouth opening in a tremulous, lopsided yawn. Not wanting him to wake up, Molly laid him gently on the bed and sat next to him for a few moments—straining to hear Lloyd's footsteps, hoping he hadn't followed her. She swallowed hard. She heard nothing but the pounding of her pulse. And then, at last, she heard the front door open and close, and she relaxed a little—thinking Lloyd had gone, yet still unsure if she was in danger.

Slowly she lowered herself beside the baby. It was too much to fathom, his trying to become intimate with her. This was a man who never missed a day of church! He studied his Bible in his radio shack every morning and was a handyman helper to the single mothers in the church—taking casseroles and food baskets to the needy! What had he meant by his questions? Had she misunderstood him? She hoped so. And yet she was dreadfully certain she hadn't.

Molly found herself staring at the door as she used to stare at the closet when she was a little girl waking from a bad dream and expecting a monster to come out of it. That was what Lloyd had become to her—a terrifying, unpredictable monster mas-

querading as a father-in-law. Yes, she had thought him obnoxious when she first met him, but she was willing to allow that
everyone is probably obnoxious to someone else at some time.
She loved Steve, and his obnoxious father was just part of the
package. But *perverted* was so much different from *obnoxious*.
Why didn't anyone else recognize this? The Bowkers had lots of
warm and loyal friends.

The door began to open slowly, and Molly froze in place until
she saw Steve's handsome, square face in the narrow opening.
"Are you awake?" he whispered.

"Oh! It's you!" Molly said, relieved. "I thought it was your
dad. Come in." At last, feeling safe, she squeezed her eyelids
tightly together to prevent the tears from starting to flow.

"Dad's outside," Steve said. "He told me you were sleeping."

"I wish," Molly said with a sigh.

"What's the matter? Has the baby been fussy?"

"No, he's been OK. I just don't like to be left alone with your
dad. Where'd you go, anyway?" She was whining, and she hated
herself for it—but she couldn't stop.

"Grandma wanted to get some wrapping paper from the
store, so I said I'd take her."

"Then I really *was* alone with him." She said it as an ominous
revelation, but Steve didn't seem to notice.

"I thought Dad was going to take the gifts to the church,"
Steve said, "or I wouldn't have left."

"No. Apparently your mom took the gifts, and he stayed
here—with me—and asked me all kinds of embarrassing questions about the baby."

"I'm sorry," Steve said, stroking her forehead. "He didn't intend them to be embarrassing, I'm sure. He's just excited about
his first grandchild and wants to know all about it."

"Well, he has no right to ask me *all* about it. If he wants to
know how it feels to give birth and to nurse a baby, he can ask
his wife." Molly's face was screwed up painfully.

There was a knock on the door, and they both jerked their
heads up—hoping no one had heard their conversation.

It was Grandma Feldman.

Grandma's dear face was wreathed in its perpetual smile.

For the wedding, she had had her snow-white hair professionally combed and twisted into a French knot at the back of her head, held in place by a row of pearl-tipped pins.

Steve stood up. "Come in, Grandma."

"I'm not interrupting anything, am I?" she asked sweetly.

"No, not a thing. Molly just put the baby down, and we were talking."

"Well, good, then. I wanted to take another peek at my first great-grandson while things are quiet, before everything starts getting busy again."

"You can sit here, Grandma." Steve indicated his place on the bed. "I'll go outside and see if I can find something to do to help."

"OK, dear," Grandma agreed. As Steve closed the door behind him, Grandma turned back to Molly. Her eyes warmed at the sight of the dark-haired baby sleeping peacefully. "He's just beautiful, Molly," she said.

"Thanks. I think so too."

"Such a new, innocent life. I was so worried when I heard it was a boy," she said, as though thinking out loud.

Molly laughed lightly. "You were? Why?"

Grandma settled herself on the bed and looked squarely at Molly, her eyes suddenly serious. "You know about Lloyd, don't you?"

"What do you mean?"

The saintly old woman kneaded her hands in her lap and looked furtively toward the closed door before going on. "It may not be my place to tell you . . . but I'm afraid that if I don't, no one else will. And I can't let the baby—"

"What is it, Grandma?" Molly urged, feeling a sudden panic as she guessed she was about to hear confirmation of something she had wanted to believe was false.

"Well, it happened a long, long time ago. I'm sure it's not a problem now, but you have a right to know. He was a teacher . . . and there was a . . . problem with some of his students."

Molly's face was stony. "What do you mean?"

Grandma cleared her throat self-consciously. "Well, it's not exactly clear, but the story was that he was getting quite personal with them, and their parents were offended."

"Do you mean he—" She couldn't finish her sentence. She couldn't bring herself to say "molested." It was too awful, too evil to say. Somehow, if she didn't call it "molesting," it was easier to deal with. Lloyd didn't look like a child molester.

"How many students did he get 'friendly' with?" Molly asked hesitantly.

"Twenty. Thirty. I can't remember now. Mostly boys. Someone reported him, and he lost his teaching certificate and his right to live in that state. But he was never convicted."

"Really?" Molly's head was reeling. "When did this happen?"

The matriarch waved the question away. "It was years ago—before Lloyd and Barbara were married."

"Did Barbara know about it?"

"She knew. But Lloyd said he hadn't meant to hurt them; he felt he was nurturing them—showing affection. He said he had been misunderstood. Barbara was sure he would never do anything harmful to his own children, and Lloyd was so crushed and embarrassed by the gossip going around that Barbara felt he needed some support. She was afraid he would kill himself if she broke their engagement."

Molly marveled at how much like Barbara she was in her support of the underdog.

"So they got married anyway?"

"Yes. And moved to Canada for a couple years, till the dust settled."

"And . . . did he hurt his own children?"

"We don't know for sure. Barbara denies it. Whenever they visited me, I tried to look out for Steve and Patti and the twins."

Molly's stomach twisted. "Do you think he'll hurt Teddy?"

"I don't think so. But I thought you should know the history so you don't change the baby's diaper in front of him. Just be on guard; don't let him take the baby anywhere alone."

Molly nodded. "Does Steve remember anything?"

"I don't know, honey." She smiled charmingly and placed a warm hand over Molly's. "I've frightened you, and I didn't mean to. It was years ago that this happened, dear. But this little baby is too precious to go unguarded. And," she said with a defiant lift of her chin, "I don't care if Barbara or Stu finds out

I told you. I decided I was going to break the silence and say something. If I hadn't and then heard that Teddy had been hurt, I could never forgive myself."

"Thank you, Grandma," Molly said, hugging her tightly. "I think you're right; no one else would have cared enough to say anything."

Molly said nothing to Steve about Grandma Feldman's remarks that day. She was afraid it would spoil the mood of the wedding—and there was enough moodiness in the house already, with Lloyd around.

Barbara insisted that everyone eat a hearty sit-down supper that evening before they left for the wedding. "We don't want anyone fainting," she had announced in her birdlike trill. After settling Lloyd's parents and Grandma and Grandpa Feldman at TV trays in the living room, she assigned everyone else a seat at the table. Chad, one of the sixteen-year-old twins, was directed to the foot of the table. Roger, the groom, was given the place to Chad's left, and Patti and Lloyd were placed opposite Roger. Barbara sat at the head of the table, explaining that from there she could scoot out to refill the serving dishes as necessary. To her right was a chair for Molly, then Steve, and Christopher, the other twin. Molly noticed with dread that her place was directly opposite Lloyd.

When they were shown their places at the table, Roger seated Patti and then himself. In doing so, he broke a secret rule. Molly felt sorry for Roger. This family had its own set of secret rules that newcomers found out about only when they broke them. One said that people were to stand behind the seats Barbara assigned them until Lloyd approved the arrangement.

As Molly could have predicted, Patti didn't tell Roger about his "mistake." She had learned from her mother that a husband must never be corrected.

Lloyd pounced at this opportunity to embarrass the couple. "Well, I see the bride and groom are weak-kneed already; or are you afraid this is going to be your last good meal for a few years, Roger?"

Roger grinned in embarrassment, and Patti waved a feeble

remonstrance in her father's direction, saying, in a childlike voice, "Oh, Daddy. I can cook. Remember the soup I made for you?"

Lloyd guffawed, and Patti smiled apologetically at Roger. "He's just teasing," she said.

At Lloyd's bidding, the chairs were pulled from the table, and those who knew the rules settled themselves properly. Lloyd said grace in a sonorous voice and then reached out to help himself to the steaming dish of scalloped potatoes that sat in front of his place. He served Barbara to his right and doled out a serving to Patti on his left. Then he dug the spoon into the dish again and held it up in the air.

"Ahem," he said airily.

Barbara giggled, and Molly looked at them quizzically. She had been saying something to Chad at the opposite end of the table.

Lloyd boomed, "Well? Daydreaming again?"

"No. You go ahead. I can serve myself," Molly told him. Unable to smile, she held her lips in a straight line. She was not hungry anymore.

"Sure," Lloyd said in the singsong that Molly hated. It was too syrupy to be genuine—part of a role. In that moment, nearly two years of silently observing the heavy-handed way he treated his family had just come to a head for Molly. It seemed that since she had put him in his place earlier in the day, he was trying to make her look bad in front of everyone. Molly didn't know whether it was her new-mother hormones or the tension caused by the wedding and the crowd in the house that was giving her a back-against-the-wall readiness to defend herself. Or perhaps it was the revelation that Grandma Feldman had given her, that this man was truly lecherous. She had had all she was going to take. Whatever the reason for her heated emotions, she was unable to bite her tongue any longer.

"I'm not a child," Molly said, her voice quivering. "My own father lets me serve myself." She tried to smile to soften her words, but her smile didn't reach her eyes. Steve nudged her with his elbow, as though warning her not to say more.

Lloyd stiffened. "I wasn't trying to make you feel like a child," he replied. "It's apparent you aren't"—and at this, his eyes dropped to her chest. "I was just trying to be a father to you."

"Well, thank you, but I already have a father. And I prefer to serve myself." She smiled again, stiffly, and Barbara giggled.

During the meal Molly felt that she was being stared at. When she plucked up the courage to look at Lloyd, she wished she hadn't. His unblinking eyes were fastened on her face, the corners of his mouth ever so slightly turned up in a sinister fashion—as though he was enjoying some secret thought. His stare made her skin crawl, and she shivered. Hoping she could distract Lloyd, she leaned forward to share a light comment with Chad. But when she looked at Lloyd again, he was still staring at her with an unspoken dare of domination in his eyes.

"Please don't stare at me like that," Molly said firmly.

The conversation at the table stopped abruptly, and all eyes turned to look at her. She knew she had committed the crime of publicly chiding the man of the house, and she suddenly felt like running away, but she made herself appear calm.

Lloyd sneered, "Oh, my. Someone's touchy this evening." He made snorting noises as though trying to laugh with his mouth closed, but no one except Barbara joined him.

"I don't like being stared at," Molly declared. Steve nudged her again, and she frowned at him. "Well, do you?" she asked.

Barbara's shoulders began to rise as they always did when she was embarrassed at something Lloyd did and wanted to smooth things over for him. She giggled and said, "Well! Can I pass anyone more roast?"

They finished the meal in strained silence, and then Molly excused herself without asking permission—another taboo—so she could feed and dress the baby. The way everyone in the family changed their plans or swallowed their wishes in favor of Lloyd's bothered her. From the start she had refused to be bent; but her feisty spirit and willingness to speak up against him and to voice her own wishes seemed to turn him on. She knew Lloyd must be frustrated by his lack of control over her, and that thought frightened her. He was capable of anything. But she had decided she would continue to speak up for herself and her family.

As though to justify Molly's behavior, Barbara encouraged the rest of the family to do what they needed to be ready to leave for the church in half an hour. The chairs were scooted out one at a time till Lloyd was the only one left at the table. He stared at his plate glumly, his fists pushing up the jowls on each side of his jaw.

"Are you going to get ready, dear?" Barbara called to him from the kitchen.

He replied in the tones of a martyr, "No. Not yet. I'll do the dishes."

It was a glorious wedding. Patti was beautiful, and Roger was handsome as a prince and very doting. Steve, serving as one of the ushers, was kept so busy Molly didn't see much of him all evening—not even during the reception. She and Linda spent most of their time in the mother's room with their babies.

At last the excitement ended. In spite of the confrontation she and Lloyd had had at supper, Molly had given a gracious speech at the reception and presented her in-laws with the silver tray. Then Patti and Roger had left the church in a pelting shower of rice.

In the foyer of the church, as the photographer was wrapping up his electric wires and putting away his tripod, Aunt Vera called Steve aside. "Are you coming back to the house?" she asked.

"I don't know. Let me see how Molly's feeling." He found her in the mother's room, nursing the baby.

In answer to his query, she said, "I just want to go home."

"You've got dark circles under your eyes," Steve observed gently.

"Do I? I feel like it, but I was afraid to check."

"Well, everyone's leaving early tomorrow, so we should probably tell them goodbye tonight. You'll be out soon?"

"Pretty quick. Teddy's almost done."

The family were standing patiently in a quietly milling circle at the front of the church when Molly came out to say goodbye. She was exhausted. But she hugged Grandma and Grandpa Feldman warmly, and they kissed the baby's hands. Vera insisted on holding Teddy one last time, and Molly gratefully draped the sleeping baby over her arms. Vera planted noisy kisses on his forehead and exclaimed, "Oh, he's sweet enough to eat!" Aunt Louise, who was much quieter, smiled maternally and pronounced the baby "precious."

Molly noticed Barbara and Lloyd coming toward her, and she went forward to embrace her mother-in-law warmly. "It was a beautiful wedding," Molly assured her. Then, taking Barbara by the arm, she said, "Now you go home and get some sleep. You've been working too hard."

Barbara's face showed the strain getting ready for the wedding had been, though her smile was as broad as though nothing unusual had happened. Molly thought with a touch of dismay, "She has learned her lessons far too well. She would starve herself if that was what someone else wanted." Barbara was a dear, dear person who spent all her energies trying to make everything seem right in her family.

Molly turned, hoping she could slip away without having to hug Lloyd, but he suddenly loomed directly in front of her. "You're going home now?"

"Yeah. At last. I guess Steve will see you in the morning." Molly made herself smile, as Barbara would, as though nothing was amiss.

"Hey, now. I saw you hugging everyone else. You're not getting away without giving me a hug too." Lloyd's arms were wide open, his mouth gaping in a sardonic smile.

Vera returned with the baby and placed him in Molly's arms. "She can't hug you; she's got the baby now," she said jovially.

"Now, you didn't have to do that," Lloyd chided his sister-in-law.

Holding the baby to her chest, Molly stretched up to give Lloyd a peck on the cheek, hoping the baby's interference would make the hug a little less personal. But Barbara giggled and snatched Teddy from Molly's arms. "Here. I'll take the baby so you can give Dad a big hug!" Molly knew it was a conspiracy—Barbara's way of arranging a favor for Lloyd so he wouldn't be moody.

With the baby gone from her arms, Lloyd crushed Molly against himself in the way she despised, his face in her hair, his breath in her ear. "Oh, thank you," he said in a husky voice. Eventually, he released her. "You take good care of Steve now, if it's not too soon—you know what I mean." He winked.

Of all the . . . I can't believe he'd say that to me! Molly sputtered silently to herself as she climbed into the car. "Let's go," she told Steve softly out of the corner of her mouth.

Barbara had handed the baby to Steve, and he had the baby in his lap, making a big fuss of pretending Teddy was blowing goodbye kisses to the grandparents. Molly said, "I just got him to sleep, Steve. Can you stop that?"

"Be patient," Steve said, without looking at her. "We'll go when Teddy's said his goodbyes properly."

At last Steve handed the baby over to Molly and backed slowly out of the drive. "What was your problem?" he asked once they were on the highway.

"Your dad," Molly said heatedly. She wanted to add, "He gives me the creeps," but knew that wouldn't be kind. She wouldn't want Steve saying that about her own father. So she just said, "I don't like the way he hugs me so tightly and then says, 'Thank you,' as though I've done him a favor or something."

"I think he just likes you," Steve said.

"I don't think he does; I make him mad."

"Well, then that's probably why he thanks you for hugging him. It must mean, 'Thank you for not being mad.' "

"I don't know," Molly said. She couldn't bring herself to tell Steve about his father's ugly past.

CHAPTER
7

December 1972

December in Seattle, and another baby due to arrive. Molly had encouraged Steve to follow his dreams and work toward becoming a doctor. To her surprise, in 1970, the summer when Teddy was born, he had agreed, applying to the University of Washington. He had had a good grade-point average, so he had been accepted immediately. Molly and Steve had moved to Seattle, where the university was located, in the fall—when Teddy was two months old. This was their third Christmas there.

Unusually cold weather had virtually paralyzed Seattle that winter. All the houses huddled silently under a beautiful, but uncomfortable, blanket of white, and no one went out unless it was absolutely necessary.

With his hands in his pockets, Steve paced back and forth in front of their apartment window, staring down at the frozen sidewalk below. It was a beautiful sight—the glazed sidewalks reflecting the blinking blips of Christmas lights in the windows on the first floor. That is, it would have been a beautiful sight if one were wanting to see Christmas lights on a black December night. But to Steve, the sight was worrisome. Molly was in labor with their second child. In this weather, the streets would be treacherous.

He massaged the back of his neck and turned to look at Molly—who, despite being in labor, had been the one to be sure that Barbara had an afghan for her chilly legs. Now she was sitting stoically on the couch, between contractions, drawing pictures for Teddy.

With Molly's parents in Michigan, Barbara was the closest grandma. She was staying with Molly and Steve so she could look after Teddy if Molly went into labor at night. While she waited, she was crocheting Christmas decorations for their apartment—a white-and-green Christmas tree that stood fifteen inches tall, and a Mr. and Mrs. Snowman dressed in winter clothing.

A quick glance at the cuckoo clock above the piano revealed that it was just seven o'clock; the night was young. Molly's voice came from somewhere deep in the couch. "Come over here and sit down, Steve. Quit your pacing. You're a third-year premed student—you should know that everything's going fine."

She turned to Barbara. "He never has been able to relax and just sit still. He's always got to be moving, doing something. Come on, Steve, sit down. Relax."

Steve turned back to the window. "Everything's going fine with you, yes. It's the driving I'm worrying about."

"Then let's go now, and you can drive slowly."

Barbara chirped, "I'll put Teddy to bed. You go on. Just call me as soon as it's born."

"Thanks, Mom," Steve said, giving her a perfunctory kiss on the cheek and a squeeze of the arm. He hauled Molly to her feet. As she stood, an unexpected gush of water poured down her leg.

For a moment she stared at the green-tinged fluid disappearing into the carpet; then she found her voice. "Uh oh. It's green. Didn't they tell us in childbirth classes that it's not supposed to be green?"

"Oh, great. Now we've got to hurry after all," Steve said. He was racing around the room like a Keystone Cop, gathering towels and blankets.

"What are you doing?" Molly asked him. "Let's go."

"Listen—if I have to deliver this baby in the car, I want to be prepared," Steve said.

Barbara laid aside her crocheting and stood as though to guide them to the door. "Go on, go on. Everything's going to be all right. Just call me when it's here. I'll say a prayer."

"Thanks." Molly gave her a quick hug before Steve ushered

her out the door in front of him. "Teddy's been doing pretty well with his potty-training," she called out as an afterthought. "Just make sure he goes potty before bed and put training pants on him, not diapers."

"OK. We'll be fine. Don't worry," Barbara said with a smile.

Teddy waved and returned to his coloring, happy to be with his grandma.

It was all over within an hour. Steve called his mother from Molly's room. "We got here just in time," he said. "The doctor didn't make it, but the nurse caught it half an hour after we walked in the doors."

"I thought she'd go fast. What is it, by the way?"

"It's a boy!" Steve's voice cracked with excitement. "Another boy—but we're happy. Seven pounds even. We're naming him Jerry." Steve was exhilarated. "I'll call Dad."

At those words, Molly felt a hot band of tension tighten around her chest. The realization that this baby's grandpa was a child molester cast a dark shadow on this moment of supreme joy. Molly still didn't want to believe it. Lloyd was so good with Teddy, and Teddy loved being with him. How could he be such a good grandpa if he were a child molester? And now they had made another potential victim.

Steve was still on the phone to his mother. He told Molly, "Teddy wants to talk to you."

"Is he still up?"

"He heard the phone ring."

"OK then." There was a pause, and then Teddy's little voice came on the line.

"Teddy?" Molly said gently.

"Mommy!" the toddler shrieked.

"Hi, honey. You have a new brother. His name is Jerry." Smiling, she paused to listen. "Mommy will be home tomorrow. I love you." She held the phone out to Steve. "He wants to talk to you now."

Listening, Molly smiled and kissed the top of the baby's blond head. She imagined Teddy nodding solemnly, as he often did when someone was talking to him on the phone. Then he would bound away, letting the receiver drop with a clunk to the table.

Just then, Steve winced and jerked the phone from his ear.

"He dropped it?" Molly asked with a soft laugh, and Steve nodded wryly in the affirmative.

Steve stayed a little longer with Molly and his new son. Then, saying a reluctant goodbye, he left for home.

It was some time before Molly fell asleep. Now she had two little boys to protect from Lloyd. If Grandma Feldman voiced her suspicions, they must be true. She wouldn't make up a story like that unless she had some sort of personal vendetta against her son-in-law. Was that possible? No. Not for a woman of Grandma's character. What she had said must be true; and yet, Molly didn't want it to be. She had to take it seriously, though. And Steve should know. Especially now, with Teddy's potty-training going on. Lloyd must not help with that. Telling Steve would be difficult, but he had to know about Grandma's warning.

There was, however, no good time to tell Steve. Barbara was staying with them for a week, and then Molly's mother was flying in from Michigan. Steve wouldn't want to discuss the issue while his mother was there. And Molly didn't want to discuss it with her mother there the next week.

At last, the mother-in-law visits were over. Now Molly began preparing for their annual Christmas visit with Barbara and Lloyd. If Molly had not insisted that they spend Christmas with the Bowkers for Teddy's sake, they would never have gone. Going was always her idea; Steve just acquiesced.

Now, even though Jerry had just arrived, Molly wanted Teddy to enjoy this Christmas with his grandparents, so she began making plans. She felt her boys were safe there because she was so vigilant and checked on them so frequently. And the rumors were about such a long time ago, anyway. Perhaps Lloyd no longer did that kind of thing.

But she still had not found the opportunity to discuss with Steve the problem of protecting the boys from Lloyd. Steve needed to concentrate on preparing for his exams, which occupied him almost right up to Christmas. Finally, the night before they left on the long drive to Crescent City, Molly found the courage to talk about the secret she had not shared with anyone during the past two-and-a-half years.

The apartment was silent except for the soft click of the Christmas lights around the window in their bedroom. Outside, the tires of an occasional passing car hissed on the wet pavement. In the semi-darkness, Molly pulled the sheets up to her neck and cradled her head in her hands while she watched the blinking lights.

Steve's back was to her. He shifted his shoulders and re-adjusted his head on the pillow. "What's wrong?" he asked in a muffled voice. "You should be sleeping."

"I can't."

"Well, you should, while the baby's quiet."

"I know. I'm just thinking."

"About what?"

"It's something I haven't wanted to believe for a couple of years. It's about your father."

"Oh, no." Steve sighed loudly and rolled onto his back. "What is it this time?" There was an edge of irritation to his voice.

"It's something Grandma Feldman told me when Teddy was born. I didn't want to upset you, so I didn't say anything. But I think it's time we talked."

"Well, what is it?"

Molly closed her eyes a moment and tried to muster up some strength. When she opened them again, she spoke toward the ceiling. "Grandma Feldman said there was a problem with your father and some children several years ago."

"What kind of problem?"

"Getting too personal with them."

"So?"

"So, she said we shouldn't change Teddy's diaper in front of him and shouldn't let him take Teddy anywhere alone. You may have noticed I've been careful about that."

"I hadn't noticed, actually."

"Whenever we go there, you stay outside as much as you can," Molly said with a touch of annoyance. "Why don't you ever come inside and sit with me while we visit?"

"I don't know. But what does that have to do with this?"

"I don't want you to let your father take Teddy to the bathroom while we're there. It's got to be either you or me who takes him. If you can't take him when he needs to go, I'll take him even if I have to stop nursing Jerry to do so. OK?"

"I guess."

Steve was shrugging the whole thing off. Molly sat up quickly, and the sheets crackled loudly in the quiet room. Somehow she had to get him to realize how serious she was. Her voice grew stern. "Steve. This is important, and you've got to help me. Your dad has hurt a lot of children—maybe even you. And I don't want it to happen to my kids. If we find out later that it's not true, I won't regret that I took precautions. But I couldn't live with myself if I shrugged it off and he hurt my boys."

"OK. OK." Steve was trying to placate her. "I'll take Teddy whenever I can. But I don't like to do it. And since I'm not in the house a lot, you're asking for a lot of work."

"I don't care. I'll do it. I'll do anything to protect my boys from your father."

Steve groaned like an animal in pain and ran his fingers through his hair. "Molly, you're talking about the boys' grandpa here. He's not going to hurt them. He loves them!"

"He loved you too. And he may have hurt you."

"I don't remember anything happening. I mean he's obnoxious, yes; demanding and arrogant sometimes. But I don't remember being actually abused." Steve lay unmoving for several seconds, as though trying to remember. "I mean, there were the spankings on my bare bottom with a hanger. And when I was in high school, he asked me if there were any boys in the dorm who . . . played with each other."

Steve groaned. "There *was* something. I haven't thought about this for a long time, Molly. I'm surprised I remember it, but I do—too clearly. When I was maybe eight years old, Dad took a bunch of boys from the church camping. Dad was the only adult with us. We went for a hike, and I was so embarrassed because we had to go to the bathroom, but he wouldn't let us stop hiking. Finally he stopped us on the steepest part of the trail." Steve sat up slowly and drew his legs in, hugging his knees to himself. His voice fell as the painful memory became fresh again. "I was so embarrassed. Dad insisted that we see who could shoot his urine farthest over the bank . . . he was watching us all with our pants down . . . he was the only one enjoying himself."

"I hope that's the worst of what he did to you," Molly said tonelessly.

"I don't know. That was uncomfortable, but I wouldn't actually call it abuse."

"If it makes you feel uncomfortable, it is abuse." Molly was firm. "That's why we need to protect our boys. We don't want them to have painful, repressed memories."

Steve opened his arms, and Molly slid over to let him hold her. Together they lay down again, and Steve caressed the top of her head with his lips. "They're so lucky to have you for a mother."

"And you for a dad," Molly added.

The next day, when Steve and Molly drove into the Bowkers' driveway, a Christmas carol was offering its cheer through the car radio. Seeing the lights of the Christmas tree blinking from the window of Steve's parents' home, Molly turned to him with a radiant smile. "Oh, Steve, isn't that a cheery scene? I just love Christmas."

Steve nodded somewhat apprehensively. "Enjoy it while you can."

Molly knew what he meant. Moments of friction came interspersed with the good times. Molly usually blamed her outspokenness for the problems and tried to guard against them. But still, they came.

Barbara appeared at the door with a red Christmas pantsuit on, her white organdy apron tied perkily around her waist. Her arms were open. "Hi! Come in. How was your trip?"

"Hi, Grandma!" Teddy squealed, jumping into her arms.

Lloyd took him out of her arms and dragged him back to the car. "You get your shoes out of there, little boy, and put them on." He spanked him playfully on the behind.

Eager to please, Teddy crawled back into the car and hauled out his tennis shoes. He stuck a foot out the door. "But they don't fit over my jammies." He held out his arms. "Carry me, Grandpa."

"Well, OK."

With Teddy deposited in the living room, Lloyd returned to help unload the car so Molly and the baby could stay inside.

They had a good visit that evening. Molly thought if she were writing a diary, she would make this entry: "Unusual evening. No tensions tonight."

In the morning Lloyd suggested to Teddy that he take a bath in the tub and make lots of bubbles so he could take pictures. Molly agreed to part of the suggestion. "We don't need the pictures, but I'm sure Teddy would love a bubble bath." She explained to Lloyd, "We don't have a tub in our apartment."

"Then this is his first bubble bath?"

"No, he had a bubble bath at Linda's before they moved away."

"But that's been six months ago—or more," Lloyd objected.

"Well," Molly offered, "if you really want pictures, I'll take some for you, and you can see them when I get them developed."

Lloyd's eyes grew dark. "You can take your own pictures if you want—but not with my camera." His voice was stern.

"*I* don't need pictures," Molly said lightly, attempting to brighten the mood. "He'll just have the bath."

Teddy was watching the exchange of words like a spectator at a tennis match, his little head turning from one face to the other, a confused expression in his eyes. "I want bubbles!" he said.

"OK!" Molly said with excitement. "Let's go make bubbles for you."

"Will you watch me swim?"

"You bet!"

"And Grandpa?"

"No. Just Mommy." She tried to sound matter-of-fact.

Teddy began whining, "But I want Grandpa to watch me too."

Without giving Lloyd a chance to reply, Molly said, "Grandpa has other things to do. Mommy will watch you swim. Come on!"

Lloyd turned soundlessly with slumped shoulders and went out to his radio shack. He had built the shack, really just a room in the garage, with the help of Marty Duncan, one of the young fathers in the church he and Barbara attended. Marty and his wife Teresa had four children, their two boys only a couple years older than Teddy and Jerry.

Lloyd spent most of his days off in his radio shack. It was a yellow room, long and narrow, with avocado-green carpeting on the floor and desk-type counters along each wall. Being in the room made Molly claustrophobic, for there was barely enough room to turn around. Drawers under the counters were full of papers, pens, and manuals and floppy disks for the computer Lloyd had just purchased. On the counter were cabinets, which held screws, nails, and other mechanical necessities. But the main objects in the room were his ham radio and his computer.

Lloyd prided himself on being one of the first ones in his church to own a computer, and he took delight in showing it off to everyone who was invited over to visit. The computer was limited, however, in what it could do, and Lloyd's explanation of its use was so boring that the adults tired of it fairly quickly. While the adults wandered out, Lloyd would usually put on a game children could understand, and, hauling a child onto his lap, would begin to play the game. Molly was aware of this practice and made a point of checking on the situation often whenever she was there while other families' children were visiting. She would be even more alert now that Teddy was at an age when he might be out there too.

The family attended a choral program at church that evening. Before the program, Lloyd paraded Teddy through the halls, holding him close to his heart, showing him off to as many people as he could find. They all seemed delighted to see the little boy again and warmly welcomed Molly and Steve back. Molly was happy to see her college roommates, Vicki and Leona, there as well. They were visiting their families during the holidays.

Leona had warmed over the years. As Molly had become familiar with Lloyd's unsettling personality, she had written to Leona, expressing her agreement with Leona's comment years before that Lloyd was weird. Now Molly seemed to be on the "other side" from Vicki, who stuck up for the Bowkers in her usual loyal way. Her own children, she had written, knew the Bowkers better than Molly's boy did. And Vicki and her husband had so appreciated the Bowkers keeping their son for a long weekend while they got away for a "second honeymoon." There was no need for an explanation; Vicki knew why Molly and Steve felt they had to keep their distance, but Vicki thought their reasons were unsubstantiated.

The first half of the program was nearly over when Teddy leaned on Molly's lap and whispered, "I need to go potty."

"In just a few minutes," Molly whispered back with a nod. She was nursing Jerry discreetly, sitting between Steve and Barbara.

Teddy leaned against her lap for a few seconds and then began squirming again. Steve pulled the little boy onto his lap and tried to divert his attention, but Teddy wriggled off his lap. "Potty. I need to go potty," he insisted.

"It's almost done," Steve whispered.

Barbara leaned forward with a smile and held out her hands to Teddy. Grinning, he headed for her, stumbling over Molly's feet. In her lap, he leaned up and pulled her ear down to his face. "Potty." Molly could hear the word plainly.

"Shall I take him?" Barbara offered quietly.

Deciding that letting her take him out would be less distracting than the squirming and whispering he would be doing if she made him stay, Molly agreed gladly. She glanced down at Jerry and then looked up again—to see Lloyd stand to his feet and lead Teddy toward the aisle. She nudged Steve urgently. "Your dad's taking Teddy to the bathroom. Hurry."

"Sh. What do you want me to do?" Steve hissed.

"Go after him. Don't let him take him."

Steve turned to look at the back doors of the church. Molly knew he didn't like to make a scene and would not follow his dad. She was not surprised when Steve whispered, "It's too late. He just went into the foyer. It's fine."

Molly's stomach knotted. Her throat was suddenly dry, and she felt a white-hot streak of tension shoot from her neck to her toes. Her breath became shallow. Quickly releasing the baby, she put herself together, pulled her jacket across her chest, and hurried to the doors through which Lloyd and Teddy had just disappeared. She ran toward Lloyd with difficulty, the heels of her shoes catching in the carpet. She never addressed Lloyd and knew he would pretend not to hear her if she called his name anyway. So she called Teddy. He turned immediately and stopped. Lloyd stopped momentarily, as though puzzled. When he saw Molly, his face froze in an icy stare.

Molly held out her hand. "*I'll* take him," she said firmly. She said it without anger; it was just a statement of fact.

Lloyd offered grandly, "I'd be happy to take him."

"I know it, and thank you. But I thought Barbara was going to take him. And since she can't, I will."

Teddy couldn't wait any longer. Seeing that, Molly held open the door to the women's restroom, and they went in. Teddy didn't really need any help. He could do the whole procedure alone.

While he finished, Molly leaned against the counter. Her legs were shaking, and torrents of confusing emotions clashed inside her. Steve had promised to be vigilant against Lloyd. Why had he refused to get up and take Teddy to the bathroom when she asked him to? And Barbara. She had offered, and Molly had gratefully accepted. However inadvertently, by transferring Molly's permission to Lloyd, Barbara had nearly undermined the defenses Molly had established. She felt she was in a one-woman battle against them all.

Was her vigilance really necessary? Somehow she felt that it was.

CHAPTER
8

1975

Molly and Steve spent the Christmas of 1974 in Michigan with Molly's parents. Their family room, sunk two steps below the rest of the main floor, was a light and airy room surrounded by wide windows that showed off a pristine view of winter. It was a comfortable room that said "family" in every sense of the word, with soft, welcoming furniture in pastel blue and peach. On nearly every wall, Kate had arranged clusters of family photos, pictures Molly and Linda had drawn as little girls, and shadow boxes of their favorite toys and baby booties. Every morning the snow revealed new tracks coming out of the forest, the trails of light-footed rabbits looking for food. Molly threw out chunks of bread and apple slices each evening before she went to bed, and they were always gone by morning.

Teddy, four and a half, and two-year-old Jerry were absolutely enamored with the snow. Grandpa Spencer made a snow cave for them. And on the afternoon of Christmas Eve, he took everyone to a nearby hill for sledding. Afterwards, they enjoyed hot chocolate and doughnuts before opening presents.

That holiday with Molly's parents was such a pleasant one. The only nerve-jarring incident occurred when Jerry, running through the house, knocked the umbrella stand against the French doors. Everyone had cringed, waiting for the sound of breaking glass. Fortunately, it never came.

In spite of the relaxed mood, Steve was unable to sit still. He seemed preoccupied, but when asked about it, he couldn't put his finger on any specific anxieties. One night, while he was sitting on the brick hearth beside the crackling fire, he confessed his restlessness to his father-in-law.

Brad said, "Well, maybe you don't have to have a problem in order to feel restless. You've been under a lot of pressure, son. You've got two boys and a wife to look after, in addition to your schoolwork. I'm sure it hasn't been easy."

Steve nodded, dropping his head. He massaged the back of his neck and stretched grandly. "Maybe that's it. It's beginning to feel like an endless road—especially since I'm taking it slower than normal."

"I'm sure it does. But you just keep on keeping on. You can do it, I'm sure."

"That's good to hear. I wish my father encouraged me like that."

"Doesn't he?"

"Naw. He never has. He's always been a pessimist." Steve chuckled. "Half the reason I'm doing this is to prove him wrong. He says I'll never be a doctor, that I don't have the self-determination to keep at it. He says I'll never be as good as the other doctors because my attitude is wrong. When I played the piano and made mistakes, he always said I should be ashamed. And I *was* ashamed—until Molly taught me to let the mistakes go. Dad sees doing that as laziness. Any performance that isn't perfect is grounds for criticism and a lecture." Steve shook his head as though to shake off the memory. "I'm so glad that's behind me now."

"I remember the college talent show," Brad said. "Kate and I were shocked that he came down so hard on you for missing one note, when we thought you had played beautifully."

"Yeah. And when he said that, he was controlling himself for your benefit." While Steve was talking, he had begun jamming his fingers together in a tent shape. Now he sat silently for a minute, studying his hands. When Brad didn't speak, he continued. "I don't know. I always felt like I had to do a perfect job to somehow bring dignity to the family—like it was all on my shoulders. And if I made a mistake, I was told in no uncertain terms that I had brought them shame."

"Well," Brad said, "we're awfully proud of you, Steve."

"Thanks. Molly and I want things to be different for our kids."

"Good for you. You can do it. Don't worry about competing with other people; just try to do the best you can. Maybe you won't finish at the top of your class—but just by graduating, you'll be accomplishing what a lot of people never have. And that's something to be proud of! You're going to make it! And we're going to be in the audience with our buttons popping off when you graduate—you can count on that!"

"Thank you," Steve said with a shy smile.

That Christmas vacation ended too soon. Steve, Molly, and the boys returned to Seattle and settled comfortably back into their lives.

That summer, Brad and Kate drove out for a visit—which the boys enjoyed as much as Steve and Molly did.

Christmas soon rolled around again. Steve hadn't wanted to spend another Christmas with his folks, but here he was in Crescent City again, being a benevolent son because Molly insisted on it.

"And here's a gingerbread man for Teddy to hang on the tree." Grinning, Barbara dangled a stuffed Christmas tree ornament in front of the little boy. He was five and a half now, the oldest of the three grandsons who had been added to the Bowker family in three consecutive years. Patti and Roger had a son, whom they had named Ryan, the year after Teddy was born—almost nine months from the day of their wedding. They had both been struggling through community college since then.

But the years had flown by swiftly. Jerry was already three years old; he was no baby. Molly had been trying to protect the boys from Lloyd without telling them about his past. She hoped to avoid coloring their impressions of Lloyd; they loved him so much. But it was during this Christmas visit that Molly realized with horror that she had waited just a little too long.

Lloyd had been acting peculiar off and on during the entire long weekend. Then, on Sunday morning, Molly, who always kept herself within earshot when Lloyd and her boys were together, heard Lloyd suggest that Teddy lie on top of him. She hurried into the living room from the kitchen just as Teddy dropped his toys and lay tummy to tummy on top of Lloyd, resting his head on his grandpa's chest. Lloyd's eyes were closed, and he was smiling a self-satisfied sort of smirk.

"Teddy, you're too big to lie on top of Grandpa," Molly stated sternly.

"Oh, no, he's fine," Lloyd said in a dreamy voice. His arms were clasped at Teddy's waist, and he pressed the boy's hips tighter to his pelvis.

"No, he's too big. He doesn't need to do that," Molly said firmly. "Get off, Teddy."

The little boy raised his head and looked from one adult to the other with a puzzled expression.

Molly held out her hand. "Come here, Teddy. Let Grandpa sit up. Maybe he can read a book to you or something. Do you want to choose one for him?"

While Teddy skipped down the hall, Lloyd continued to lie unmoving on the couch. He opened his eyes and stared up at the ceiling. Seeing that he wasn't going to look at her, Molly returned to the kitchen to help Barbara with the dishes. In a few moments she heard Teddy giggling in the living room, and she moved over to the table where she could see him while she put the silverware away in the drawer. Lloyd was standing up, helping Teddy to do flips to the floor. "Grandpa! Remember when we touched tongues?" Teddy said loudly with a giggle.

Molly's eyes narrowed as Lloyd shot her a guilty glance and then looked away, smiling desperately at the little boy. "That was only playing," he explained with an uncomfortable chuckle. "We were just passing an almond back and forth from your lips to mine." Lloyd glanced at Molly again, furtively, as though wondering if she had bought his explanation. Barbara fumbled with a pile of papers on the counter, giggling self-consciously.

"Come here, Teddy," Molly said. Her voice was very serious, and the little boy's face fell. She took his hand gently and led him down the hall, feeling as though her stomach were filled with ice-cold water. It was time to tell Teddy the ugly truth about his Grandpa Lloyd. Lloyd was making her do this, and once more Molly felt nauseating, helpless anger toward him for it.

Teddy sat crouched like a thin cat in a corner of Patti's pink-checked canopy bed, and Molly's heart ached for him. He was so little. She almost changed her mind and kept the secret to herself, so uncertain was she that this was the right thing to do. She had held food in her lips for Teddy too—graham crackers, mostly. It was a game they played, and it always ended with a kiss on the lips. What if that was all Lloyd was really doing?

On the other hand, what if this were only the beginning of his indiscretions with her son? She had to arm Teddy with knowledge so he could protect himself if necessary. Now that he was older, he didn't like staying as close to her as he had before. He was more on his own now. He needed information, and he needed her permission to tell his grandpa No.

Molly tried to be vague as she broke the awful secret to her son. She sat down beside him and wrapped him in her arms. "Honey, Grandpa loves you very, very much," she began. "But there are good ways and bad ways to show people that we love them." He looked up at her with round, innocent eyes framed by beautiful dark lashes. She swallowed hard and continued. "A long, long time ago, before Daddy was born, Grandpa did some things with little boys and girls that he wasn't supposed to do because they didn't know they could tell him No."

"What did he do?"

"I don't know, exactly, but I just wanted to tell you that it happened so you will know. Can you tell me about the almond thing with you and Grandpa?"

Teddy rubbed a nervous palm up and down the leg of his blue jeans. "It was nothing." He shrugged. "We were just passing an almond back and forth, and Grandpa was trying to find it in my mouth with his tongue. It tickled!"

Molly felt sick. "Did that make you feel uncomfortable, like you wished he wouldn't do that?"

"Yeah. Kinda."

"Well, that was wrong of Grandpa to do that." She hesitated, her mind whirring, wondering how far to take the conversation. She decided to ask what she hoped would be denied. "Has Grandpa ever tried to look at or touch your private parts, honey?"

"No."

"Well, you know that if someone ever touches any part of you that your swimming suit covers and tells you to keep it a secret, that's 'secret touching.' And you can tell people not to touch you in that way—OK?" She was rambling and she knew it, but she couldn't help herself.

"I know." Teddy sounded insulted.

"If Grandpa ever again does anything that makes you feel uncomfortable, you have Daddy's and my permission to tell him to stop. Then it's important that you come to me and tell me what he's doing. Because even though he's your grandpa, he doesn't have the right to do any secret touching. And if he says that I'll hate you if you tell or that he'll hurt you or me if you tell—don't believe it. I will always love you, and I will never let him hurt you. And if he tried to hurt me, he would be in trouble—and he knows that." Molly touched her son's porcelain cheek with her fingertips and lifted his face to meet hers. "I love you, Teddy, and I promise to keep you safe. That's what mothers are for."

"OK. Can I go now?" the little boy asked, sliding off the bed.

Molly nodded. She sat alone on the bed for a long time afterwards, torn up inside, hoping she had done the right thing.

When she returned to the living room, she heard Teddy pleading with his grandpa to play with him, but Lloyd brushed him aside wordlessly, a frown on his face as he lumbered outside in dejected silence. It was all so confusing to Molly. Lloyd's behavior was so odd and so inappropriate, and yet he acted so hurt when that was pointed out. Molly, always one to protect the feelings of others, hated hurting him; and yet she couldn't allow the possibility of hurting Lloyd's feelings to stand in the way of protecting her boys from harm. An old proverb guided her: "For evil to prosper, good men must be silent." Molly refused to be silent. Still, she hoped fervently that she had done the right thing.

The next morning a gray rain slid down the windows, matching Molly's mood. The only thing that cheered her was the promise that they were leaving. Suspecting Lloyd of beginning a molesting relationship with her son made her feel like an ogre. And she still wasn't sure she had done the right thing by telling Teddy. Was she becoming paranoid—a rude, meddling daughter-in-law? She couldn't say anything to Steve for fear of hurting his feelings. With pain in her heart, she watched Teddy continue his attempts to patch up his relationship with his grandpa, who now acted brusque and distant to all of them.

That afternoon, as Molly collected the boys' toys from the dark living room, she felt as though she were in a fog. Lloyd and Barbara helped silently while Steve made several trips to the car with their things. Three-year-old Jerry, looking cute in his pale blue overalls and white slip-over shirt, was pointing under the couch. "My ball . . . under dere." Molly dropped to her knees and put her cheek to the floor to look under the couch. There was no ball; just some old catalogs and papers. She pulled them out, and her heart jumped when she saw that one of the catalogs featured sex toys. She leafed through it quickly, startled by the lewd pictures. Then, impulsively, she held it up to Lloyd. "What in the world are you doing with a catalog like this?" She tried to say it playfully, but she couldn't hide her shock.

The room was charged with tension. Barbara giggled and clutched the sides of her pants while she looked imploringly at Lloyd for an explanation. He shot over and snatched the catalog from Molly's hand. "Those things come all the time," he said lamely. "Junk mail." Then he made a big show of putting it in the fire.

"That's funny. I get a lot of junk mail too, but I've never gotten anything like that," Molly said. "I think you have to *request* that kind of junk mail."

Barbara piped in with a high voice, "We can't seem to stop them. We never order anything out of them, but they just keep coming."

Lloyd turned on his heels and left the room, and Barbara called Teddy and Jerry into the kitchen for a cookie. Molly sighed heavily and leaned back on her knees, resting her head on the couch. She studied the fire dancing happily behind the grate; its cheeriness seemed to mock her. The situation was becoming all too clear to her. Lloyd was a child molester. It had to be true. He was a despicable child molester operating under a very righteous cover, and Barbara was doing nothing to stop him.

And he was a church officer! Was he molesting children in the church even now? Did the church know? And if it did, why did it allow him to go on? How much longer would his secret remain protected?

At length, Molly rose to her feet and joined Barbara and the boys in the kitchen. When they finished their snack, she sent the boys out to the garage to help their daddy so she could talk with Barbara. "So you've seen those catalogs before?" she asked gently.

"From time to time."

"Have you ever looked at them?"

"Just once. But they're not just—you know—'sex toys.' They also sell bathrobes and stuff."

"Yes, they do. But I believe it's against the law for any company to send pornographic materials through the mail—and that catalog is pornographic. But they can't send that stuff out unless you request it. I would guess that Lloyd has requested that stuff."

"I don't know." Barbara looked down at the floor. Ordinarily cheerful out of necessity, she was unusually glum.

Molly guided her to a chair near the table and then pulled out a chair for herself next to her. "Barbara, I know about Lloyd. Grandma Feldman told me the weekend Patti got married—just after Teddy was born. She said she didn't know whether Lloyd had hurt Steve and the others. Do you know?"

"I'm sure he never abused the kids. But that other—what Grandma Feldman told you about—that all happened a long, long time ago."

"I know it did, but it happened. And it could happen again. That's why I've been so protective of Teddy and Jerry. It broke my heart to tell Teddy—I didn't want to have to pollute his mind. But I felt I had to do it for his own protection. They weren't just passing an almond back and forth, Barbara. Lloyd was putting his tongue into Teddy's mouth to try to 'find' the almond! Lloyd was French-kissing my son!"

Barbara shifted in her seat. She arranged her fingers like a tent, finger to finger, studying them with unblinking eyes, and Molly realized where Steve had acquired the habit.

"Can't you see what's happening, Barbara? The catalogs . . . and the picnics on which Lloyd gets 'lost' with a little boy? How many times has he gone to that same park? He should know the trails well enough by now that he doesn't get lost!"

"I don't know." Barbara traced a design on the tablecloth with one finger. "He's a good man. He has a very warm heart. He would give the shirt off his back to someone in need. I guess from time to time I have thought something was wrong with him. But he can't help it. He was abused by a farmhand when he was six. He can't help it."

"He *can* help it, Barbara. That excuse is just a cop-out. Lloyd needs therapy," Molly said. "He's just using the abuse story to get your sympathy. Lots of people have been abused who *don't* repeat the abuse. In fact, most abuse victims become 'helpers'— teachers, nurses, pastors, and the like. Steve has learned in medical school that most victims do not automatically abuse; they help others. Lloyd has *chosen* to abuse, and if he doesn't get therapy, I'm afraid he will choose to abuse one of his own grandchildren."

"I've suggested therapy, but he won't go. Says he's not sick— that people are just trying to get him. He says that he's just showing the children affection."

"Molesting is not affection, Barbara. He's sick—dangerously so. And he treats you really badly. A husband shouldn't be cutting his wife down all the time like he does."

"Oh, he doesn't mean it."

"Yes, he does mean it, and you don't deserve it. You've put up with it for too long. Have you ever thought of leaving?"

"Many times."

"Then why haven't you?"

Barbara sighed and looked down at her hands. "I talked to a pastor about this years ago. He helped me see that I can't leave. I made a solemn promise before God that I cannot break. I promised to stay with Lloyd in sickness or in health, and that includes now, when he's sick."

"There are different kinds of sicknesses, Barbara," Molly said, desperately reaching for words. "This kind of sickness is an abusive one, and you shouldn't feel like you're trapped here in this marriage with this man.

"Remember, those marriage vows are not the words of the Lord—they were made up by humans. They are wonderful vows and should be kept in most situations. But marriage is not supposed to be a sentence for abuse. No one in an abusive relationship should be made to feel like she has to stay and 'take it' because of those human vows. Barbara, God isn't going to condemn you for realizing you made a mistake you must correct by leaving Lloyd. He may have committed adultery with children!"

"But I can't leave," Barbara said sadly. "I'm all he's got. He would kill himself if I left."

The car's horn beeped, and Molly looked toward the door. "Gotta go," she said gently. "But please think about what I said. Your kids would support your choice to leave."

Barbara followed her to the garage. Lloyd had sequestered himself in his radio shack and refused to come out because of what Molly had said. Molly preferred it that way, though she didn't like stirring up trouble—even when it was justified.

Steve came around the car to give his mother a hug. "Tell Dad goodbye," he said, kissing her. Barbara had found her resiliency and waved gaily from the door as though nothing out of the ordinary had happened.

The hum of the engine put the boys to sleep quickly. While they slept, Molly told Steve about her conversations with Teddy and with Barbara. "She never told me whether he abused you," Molly said. "Do you still not remember anything?"

Steve shook his head. "I don't think he would abuse his own kid."

CHAPTER
9

November 1979

For four years, life moved along fairly routinely. Having finished medical school at the University of Washington, Steve was now taking an internship in family practice in Kansas. With both boys in school, Molly had begun working half-time in the registrar's office of the university near where they now lived. Since she was eligible for a discount on tuition, she began taking classes toward a nursing degree. And one Sunday a month, she worked at the hospital as a volunteer. She enjoyed the unpredictability of the hospital environment.

On a day Molly would never forget, a patient was admitted to the medical floor with back pain. All the staff seemed to know who Mr. Bryant was. As she assembled his chart at the nurses' desk, Molly asked Donna, one of the nurses with whom she felt comfortable, "Has he been in a lot, or something? You all seem to know his whole history."

"He's been in too much," Donna replied. "He's my ex. And he's sick in the head."

"His mind is causing his back pain?" Molly asked, snapping open the chart to fasten the pages into place. She paused and looked up at Donna for an explanation.

"He's addicted to Demerol," Donna said. "He's got sores on his legs from years of injections. I tried to help him quit, but he didn't want my help. He refuses to talk to anybody about what's eating him up inside and making him do this. When I realized that I couldn't do anything for him and that he was making *me* sick, I decided that for the sake of my kids and my finances, I had to leave him. He's still not better."

"Oh, I'm so sorry," Molly said, returning her eyes self-consciously to her work. "Has it been a while since you split up?"

"It's been ten years."

"You seem so comfortable talking about it."

"It was tough at first, and I didn't know how I'd get through. But I made it. And I can talk about it. He and I are still friends for the children's sake."

"How did you manage?" Molly wondered aloud, trying to imagine raising her two boys alone.

"It was tough. But I'm a Christian, Molly, like you. Jesus got through Gethsemane and His trial one moment at a time. And I've learned that just as He did for Jesus, God gives us strength just when we need it. Not before, not after—but *just when we need it.*

"I believed the strength would come, and it did. It came. Not before the split. Not even every morning. But moment by moment . . . as I lived each day." She closed her eyes and recited slowly, " 'When thou passeth through the waters . . . I will be with thee.' "

Molly often thought back to that conversation and Donna's wise words. It was true. God had given her strength one moment at a time as she had dealt with Lloyd and Barbara and then the move to Kansas. They had known no one in Kansas when they had moved there two years before, but things were different now—thanks to Chad's fiancée, Paige, who was a Kansas native. Chad, a junior in college majoring in physical therapy, had met Paige at the hospital two years before when he had come to visit Molly and Steve. Molly enjoyed her young brother-in-law and was delighted when he introduced her to Paige. She was a nursing student, the sort of ebullient person that shy Chad would like. Quiet though Chad was, there were no silences when he and Paige were together. She kept him regaled with side-splitting stories of her adventures in the hospital, the blond ponytail that perched high on her head swinging from side to side as she chatted away.

Molly had quickly come to love her. With Linda and Kevin away in Chicago, Paige became the sister-friend whom Molly needed. And this Thanksgiving weekend Chad would officially add Paige to the Bowker family. She would make a welcome addition.

Paige had grown up comfortably in a large home in the country, her family sharing their bounties with three foster children—a girl and two boys. One of the boys, Rick, was Teddy's age, and the two had become fast friends the first time they met. Cody, the other boy, was eleven. He was shy and retiring, and Molly didn't know him very well. Neither was she familiar with the girl, Beth—also eleven—who stayed in her room most of the time when visitors came.

Paige seemed to take Lloyd's eccentricities in stride, pleasantly putting him in his place when he became obnoxious. Her father owned a plumbing supply store, and from him she had learned excellent public relations. She handled pressure well too. Even though she was the bride, she was the one who had made sure everyone was settled comfortably in rooms she had chosen for them in the rambling farmhouse where her family lived.

Molly and Steve had been given one of the attic bedrooms. When Molly looked at the little white tuxedo that Teddy was to wear in Chad's wedding, she couldn't help smiling. Could he be nine years old already? The tux was just a warning that soon he would be a teenager, and then a grown man. This thing called life seemed to be passing so swiftly. Already it was the last Thanksgiving of the seventies.

A light knock sounded on the door. Molly ducked her head under the slanted ceiling as she crossed the room. But when she opened the door, no one was there. She looked down the narrow hall, illuminated by regularly spaced yellow cones of light, but the thin, maroon carpet revealed nothing of whoever had knocked on the door.

Guessing it was some sort of a prank, Molly called out cheerfully, "Yoo-hoo. Who's there? Is it Johnny Spineless?"

At first, there was no answer. But then Beth's curly brown head appeared just over the top of the narrow stairwell, split by a wide grin.

Molly asked, "Are you Johnny Spineless?"

Beth giggled. "Who's that?"

"You know—the guy who closes the door when nobody's there or opens it without leaving a trace."

Beth giggled again. She nodded, and Molly laughed too.

"Do you want to come in?" Molly invited. "I was just checking Teddy's tuxedo for wrinkles before going down for supper. Do you have a special dress for the wedding?"

Beth nodded. Finally she spoke, but it wasn't in answer to Molly's question. Instead, Beth asked, "Where's Cody?"

Molly answered, "I don't know, honey"—and just then the little quartet of Teddy and Rick, Jerry and Ryan, came clomping up the stairs. Teddy, hearing the question, said, "Cody went for a walk with Grandpa."

"Where'd they go?" Molly asked.

"I dunno. Down to the creek, I think."

"The creek? It must be frozen! It's cold out there! Why don't you go and tell Grandpa and Cody to come back."

Molly invited Beth to come into her room and visit. "I don't have any girls, and I'd love to talk to you."

Beth seemed pleased to fill a need. Shyly pulling herself off the stairs, she came into the room. She pointed to a dark brown, antique dresser with porcelain drawer pulls and a linen dresser scarf that hung over the ends. "I have pretty ponytail holders in the music box," she said. "Do you want to braid my hair?"

"I'd love to!" Molly exclaimed.

"Paige braids my hair when she's home. But she's busy right now—with Chad."

"I know. They're getting married tomorrow. Isn't it exciting?"

Beth looked cherubic with light, airy ringlets around her face and a red ribbon at the end of each braid. Molly was just tying the last ribbon when Steve whistled from the bottom of the stairs. Then his voice echoed in the narrow stairwell: "Time for supper!"

"We're coming," Molly called back.

Ann, Paige's mother, brought a big kettle of spinach soup from the kitchen and set it down heavily in the middle of the table on the blue-checked tablecloth. Crusty loaves of French bread and platters of cheese had been placed at each end of the table.

"We can't all sit down at the table—there are too many of us. But I thought the kids could eat here, and we adults can serve ourselves and then sit in the living room," she said. She counted heads. "Where's Cody?"

"He's down at the creek with Teddy's grandpa," Beth chimed.

"I told him supper was at five-thirty." Ann seemed disturbed. "We've got to leave for rehearsal in an hour."

Heavy footsteps and a low murmur of voices sounded at the back door. Steve opened the door and announced, "They're here." Molly tensed when she saw Lloyd standing there with Cody— Lloyd wearing an oversized grin, looking like the cat that ate the canary. He had a hand on Cody's shoulder, and Cody hung the shoulder down as though hoping Lloyd's hand would slide off.

It was obvious Cody had been crying. His eyes were red and swollen, and he kept them cast down toward the floor. He was sniffling and making hiccupping noises. Lloyd guided the boy into the room and closed the door behind them.

"Why, Cody, what's wrong?" his mother asked, hurrying toward him with concern in her eyes.

"Oh, he got a little scared. The cows chased us," Lloyd explained with a lighthearted chuckle.

"He's never been scared of the cows before," Ann said. "They should have been in the barn." She shot a puzzled glance in Lloyd's direction before putting her arms around the boy's shoulders and pulling him toward her. "Why did you get scared, honey? Are you cold? Hungry?"

"He'll be OK," Lloyd cut in with a loud chuckle. "We got the cows back into the barn OK." And then, changing the subject, he rubbed his hands together and eyed the table. "Um-m-m-m. It certainly smells good." He winked at Ann and said charmingly, "But it always smells good at your table, I'm sure. Come on, Cody, you can sit by me!"

Ann wordlessly steered Cody to a seat near her, but the boy was obviously in no mood to eat. He huddled forlornly in his chair with his arms around himself, great, silent tears slipping down his cheeks. Lloyd tried some verbal sparring, but the boy wouldn't look at him. Instead, he turned his back to the table until Lloyd left the room.

Molly's eyes found Steve's, and the anguish she saw there told her that he was struggling with accepting the horrible truth that his father was a child molester. Steve's face was pale; and like Cody, he had lost his appetite. He put down his spoon and left the room, the muscles in his jaw twitching as he fought with his suspicions of what must have happened. Barbara tried to chat gaily with Ann; no one looking at her would have thought anything was wrong. But Ann was obviously finding it difficult to act as though everything was normal.

Sunday evening couldn't come soon enough for Molly. She wanted to get as far from Lloyd as possible. She was sick of looking at him; sick of seeing him brood; sick of imagining what form of perverted thoughts took shape in his mind. One thing was certain: she wouldn't suggest going to Crescent City to visit her in-laws this Christmas. From now on, they would have Christmas at home. It was time they began to establish their own traditions with the boys anyway. What better excuse to be alone over the holidays than that?

Christmas that year began with Steve and Molly's family in an unusually festive mood. It would end with its own measure of pain.

Blissfully unaware of the discovery to come, Molly French-braided a pink ribbon in her hair, pulled on her light-pink sweat suit, and, with a warm heart and a happy smile, decorated their small apartment for the holidays—taking joy in the boys' delight at the transformation. It was with a painful twinge of nostalgia that she hung the stockings Barbara had decorated for them and brought out the Christmas tree and snowman couple that Barbara had crocheted the year Jerry was born.

But Steve had built Molly's anticipation for this Christmas. He had told Molly not to open the MasterCard bill when it came because something very special had been billed on it and he didn't want her to know how much it cost. Molly had chuckled and oohed and aahed about what it could be, but promised to leave that bill for Steve to pay.

Late the afternoon of Christmas Eve, Jerry, small for a seven-year-old, snuggled warm and fragrant in Molly's lap, and

Molly pulled Teddy in beside her on the couch to read Christmas stories. Afterwards, they sat cozily with the room lights out and listened to Christmas music while they watched the twinkling, multicolored lights on the tree and in the windows. Molly breathed deeply of the tangy aroma of the evergreen boughs on the mantel. Peppermint-stick candles burned in the green centerpiece on the table, adding their own special fragrance to the warm and friendly room.

At last it was evening. The apartment smelled heavenly: fragrant garlic bread; mugs of hot chocolate with tiny, foaming marshmallows melting on the top; fresh chocolate-chip cookies; and the traditional home-made spaghetti and meatball dinner by candlelight. Molly had been working all day to prepare the special meal. Steve, collapsed on the living-room floor, had slept right through the banging of kettles and the screeching of the excited boys.

Molly wondered how he could sleep through all the noise. It didn't seem normal. But then, he fell asleep on the floor the minute he walked in the door every evening. Molly guessed the hours he kept at the hospital offered an explanation of his perpetual tiredness.

Actually, she had been worried about Steve for nearly a year. He was sleeping too much and complained all the time about how painful his knees were. During his high-school years, a skiing accident had precipitated the need for surgery. Recently, he had seen several doctors for pain pills, and they almost always obliged. Now Molly wondered aloud how it was that football players could manage to return to the game within months after their surgeries, and yet Steve's injury of years before still hurt so much that he needed pain medication for it.

"Steve," Molly called softly, setting a mug and saucer on the floor beside him. He was wearing his gray, pleated trousers and the light pink shirt she had given him for his birthday. Molly thought him even more handsome than when she had married him.

"Steve, wake up," Molly whispered. "It's time for supper, and we can't open presents till we've eaten. I don't think the boys can wait much longer."

"Huh?" Steve groaned, forcing his eyes open. "I don't want any. I'm so tired."

"Honey," Molly said with a smile, "it's Christmas Eve! Wake up! You can go to bed later." She pulled up his eyelids and teased him. "Are you in there, Steve? Come out, come out, wherever you are! I can't wait to see my special present! Wake up!"

With a sigh, Steve heaved himself to a sitting position and leaned against the couch. The boys ran over with delighted shrieks and threw themselves across his lap. "Daddy, wake up! It's time to eat!" Molly picked up the mug of hot chocolate and took it back to the table. Jerry took one of Steve's hands and Teddy took the other, and together they heaved and pulled to get their daddy up.

Steve couldn't help smiling at the sight of his sons in their red flannel pajamas leaning way back at such an acute angle. He struggled to his feet and shuffled over to the table, sitting down heavily. "Um. You've been busy," he said.

"I made your favorite supper," Molly replied, placing the platter of steaming spaghetti in the center of the table with the garlic bread and the sauce. "Hope you're hungry."

"Well, I'm not, really," Steve said apologetically.

"You never are," Molly replied wryly. "And look at you—you've lost a ton of weight. Your skin practically hangs on your bones. I think you're working too hard."

"No. I'm tough; I'll be OK," Steve assured her with a forced smile.

He was sure he would be—as long as his friend kept him supplied with the prescriptions he needed. He would have been in misery if not for the Demerol this friend kept ordering for him. He had taken it for so long now that a normal dose of 50 milligrams just didn't cut the pain; he needed 200 to 300 milligrams at a shot. Fortunately, he thought, Molly didn't know he was taking the stuff. She was a worrier. She would worry that he was addicted to it. Addicted? Not Steve Bowker! He was a medical student. He would know when he was becoming addicted—and he wasn't addicted yet!

There was that matter of $600 in charges for Demerol on the MasterCard bill. It was those charges that he hadn't wanted

Molly to see. What would he tell her when all she got for Christmas was a small bottle of perfume? She was smart enough to know the perfume didn't cost $600! And if she saw the bill and all the charges at area pharmacies, she would know something was up. He had to think of something to keep her off the track—just for her own good, so she wouldn't worry.

They ate in silence, the only sounds in the apartment the Christmas music on the stereo and the boys' incessant chatter. At last the meal was finished, the table cleared, and the dishes rinsed. The family settled around the tree to watch the boys open their presents. They each had a big stack from Barbara and Lloyd and a couple from Molly's parents. Steve and Molly had just a few: one for each other, one from each set of parents, and pictures the boys had drawn.

Molly opened her present from Steve—a bottle of her favorite "real" perfume. She had never priced it in the stores, but she was sure it cost no more than $40. A playful grin played at the corners of her mouth. "You didn't want me to see this charge on the MasterCard bill?" she asked in disbelief. Before Steve could answer, she rushed on. "Steve, it's OK. We can afford $40—for me, at least." She laughed lightly. "I wouldn't have barked to see this on the bill. You're silly."

Steve lowered his eyes and grinned shyly. "Well, actually, I had bought something else for you. But I took it back and bought this instead, because I knew you wouldn't want me to spend as much as I did on the first thing." He was lying to cover his habit, and he hated himself for it. But he couldn't be honest with her; she would be so worried.

"What was the other thing you bought?" Molly asked, her eyes dancing.

"Oh, I can't tell," Steve lied.

"Why not? You didn't spend a cent on it, and I'd like to know what you would have bought for me if money were no problem. Please?"

Steve loved the look of her when she smiled that way. She was wearing the grape-colored mohair sweater and purple plaid skirt he had loved in college. But he was insistent on keeping his secret. He had to be, for there had been no other gift, and he didn't want to weave a bigger web of lies than he already had. "No, it doesn't matter what it was. What counts is what I actually bought for you. Spray some on! I love it!"

She did and then scooted next to Steve, laying her head on his shoulder. He slipped an arm around her, enjoying the sweet fragrance of the perfume. A choir on the tape they were playing sang "Silent Night." "Let's sing," Molly whispered. They joined the choir's music, and Teddy directed them.

When the song was over, Steve's chin was down on his chest, and he was asleep again. Molly got up without disturbing him and scooped Teddy and then Jerry off the floor. "Time for you to go to bed," she whispered, giving them each a hug.

When the boys were settled in bed, she awakened Steve, and he stumbled down the hall to bed. Alone, Molly took out the bag of treats and stuffed the boys' stockings. This was not a Christmas Eve to remember. Strange, troubling thoughts fought with each other, and her stomach churned. Something was wrong with Steve. How was she going to find out what it was?

The house was dark and still—unusually still. Molly awoke with a start, rocking slowly in the waterbed, and reached behind her to feel for Steve. He was gone. He was often gone in the middle of the night, having been called to the hospital. His schedule was chaotic, and he would often explain the next morning that he had been called away. But tonight? Steve was supposed to be off! And Molly was sure she hadn't heard the phone or his beeper.

She opened her eyes and looked around the room. Seeing the golden hem of light beneath the bathroom door, Molly was reassured that Steve was home. For several minutes she dozed briefly; then she opened her eyes to see if Steve had come to bed yet. But the light was still on. Eventually, thinking Steve had been in the bathroom for an unusually long time for the middle of the night, Molly got up and knocked on the door to see if he was all right.

In a startled voice he called out sharply, "Who's there?" Something clattered to the floor.

"It's just me, Steve," Molly said sleepily. "It's two o'clock in the morning. Are you OK?"

"Oh, yeah. I've just got gas pains," Steve explained. "Be out in a minute."

Molly pulled on her light pink bathrobe and sat on the edge of the bed. The uneasiness she had known when she was around Lloyd began to burn in the pit of her stomach again, its tight fingers constricting her chest. She began to shiver, her teeth chattering. Years before, when they had visited Lloyd and Barbara two weeks after Jerry's birth, Lloyd had embarrassed Molly by calling her aside and telling her he had wiped up some blood on the floor around the toilet. "It's not from you—bleeding from the birth, is it?" he had asked in a most sickening way. "I know you're probably not finished with that yet."

Shocked, she had told him she wasn't bleeding anymore.

Now she wondered about that blood. Could Steve have been mainlining something? Was that what he was doing now? Just yesterday a doctor had mentioned that Steve had come in asking for a first-aid kit with Demerol. The doctor had said Steve told him he needed it for a week-long backpacking trip he was planning to take—just for emergencies. The doctor told Molly that when he refused to order it, Steve had seemed self-conscious and backed out of the office, lamely saying, "Well, we probably won't need it after all." Had someone else done him this "favor"?

With a pounding heart, Molly remembered Donna's husband and the painful results of his continued battle with Demerol. She struggled to switch on the lamp beside her bed, her fingers quivering like jello. As a student nurse, she knew the look in the eyes of someone who was on narcotics. She wanted a good look at Steve's eyes. While she waited, she kept praying, "Please, God. Don't let me see it there."

At last Steve came out of the bathroom, squinting at the light. "What's the matter? Why are the lights on?"

"I just wanted to make sure you're OK." Molly fastened her eyes on Steve's face as he slowly came around the bed, the long sleeves of his brown plaid robe hanging around his wrists. He always wore that robe—even on hot summer nights. He wore long-sleeved shirts to work and had even returned the short-sleeved shirts she had bought him for his birthday a few months before, explaining that doctors looked better in long-sleeved shirts because the color continued all the way down the sleeves of their lab coats.

Steve said, "Switch your light off. I'm going back to sleep."

"I will in a minute."

"Switch it off now." Steve's voice was shaky. He stood unmoving at the side of the bed.

"You can go ahead and get into bed, Steve. I'm going to the bathroom, and then I'll switch off the light."

"You're going to the bathroom?"

"Yes. Do you mind?"

"No. Go ahead. I'll get in bed later."

Molly said, "You don't have to wait for me. Take off your housecoat and get in bed. Go ahead." She waved him toward the bed.

Steve grinned that disarming grin he had and held out his arms to her. "I want a hug first. You give me a hug and go into the bathroom, and then I'll get into bed. Come on," he said in a soft voice. "Merry Christmas."

Molly walked over to where he stood and put her arms around him. As she looked up into his face, she felt as though a brick had fallen onto her chest. She recognized on his face the look she had seen in the hospital. His pupils were pinholes. Molly felt a burning behind her eyes and turned her face away from Steve's. Laying her cheek on his chest, she blinked away the great, cold tears that dropped like weights from her eyes.

Steve didn't seem to notice. He kissed the top of her head and hugged her, then turned her toward the bathroom again. "That was nice. Now go to the bathroom, and we can both get back to sleep."

"Um-hm," Molly mumbled. She knew he would be asleep before she returned. There had been no lovemaking between them in a long time; Steve was mysteriously impotent. Demerol?

In the bathroom, she closed the door softly and turned on the light. What had clattered to the floor? There was nothing apparent in front of the toilet or the sink . . . but then Molly noticed an uncapped syringe lying on the floor behind the toilet. With a shaking hand, she picked it up. A roaring noise began to build in her ears, and, realizing her trembling legs wouldn't support her much longer, she closed the toilet and sat down heavily. Deeply distraught, she alternately ran her fingers through her hair and clenched fistfuls of it as silent sobs racked her body. "Oh, God," she cried silently. "Why is he doing this? What am I going to do? How am I going to help him?"

She began to shake violently in the cold bathroom. Her teeth were chattering, and great, grieving sobs that she couldn't stop came from the very core of her being. Then she remembered what Donna had told her about receiving help for her needs. Moment by moment . . . by moment. "Strength, Lord. Please give me strength." Finally, with a moan, she heaved herself up from the toilet and turned off the light. She felt limp and lifeless. "Oh, God; oh, God; oh, God," she whimpered over and over again. "Oh, God." She wasn't taking God's name in vain; her words were an agonized prayer for strength.

Back in the bedroom, Molly blew her nose loudly, and, whimpering, crawled back into bed. She hoped Steve was not yet asleep—she needed comfort. But she should have known he wouldn't be there for her. Passed out in a drugged stupor, Steve snored loudly with his face to the wall. The Steve she once knew was gone; she realized quite suddenly that he had been gone for a long, long while. Now despair was her only companion.

CHAPTER

10

1980

January crept in, and the decade of the eighties began. Molly felt a little guilty about not seeing Lloyd and Barbara over Christmas, and yet she wondered how she could have tolerated the stress of a Christmas with them and the revelation of Steve's problem at the same time. She had confronted Steve with the syringe and told him about her conversation with the doctor, and he had sobbed like a baby and apologized for hurting her. Admitting he had a problem, Steve had started therapy. Now they were in what seemed to be a honeymoon state. Both of them felt lighthearted and optimistic about the future.

The only darkness came when thoughts of Lloyd crept in, forcing Molly to wonder about the secrets he hid behind his smug, self-righteous demeanor. Was he the reason Steve had turned to drugs? Had Lloyd abused his own son? Steve's counselor had said that drug abuse was most often the result of painful memories of some kind, that most drug abusers were trying to escape something in their past.

"When is he going to confront it?" Molly had asked the counselor.

"When it seems safe. When he feels some emotional distance between himself and his abuser. Or when his own child is about the age he was when he was abused."

Molly thought the camping-trip incident Steve had remembered several years before was certainly suspect. But it wasn't conclusive. Anyway, she wanted the whole thing to be a misunderstanding. She wanted to be proven wrong about Lloyd. Certainly he had never admitted having hurt any child, and nobody had seen any court records from the incident that was now nearly forty years in the past.

In addition to the suspicions about Lloyd, there were unanswered questions about his family. Barbara had said Lloyd had had some problems as a child. Could it be that his own father had molested him and started him on this gruesome path? Could that be why Grandmother and Grandfather Bowker never spoke of relatives? Could they have been shunned or disinherited by their families because of something Grandfather had done? Abuse Lloyd had suffered, if he had been abused, could never excuse his own acts. But it could explain what got him started on the path he had apparently traveled.

It was all too deep and too complicated. When Molly caught herself contemplating the possibilities, she stopped herself forcefully so she would not be drawn into the morass of despair the whole situation threatened her with. But she could never finally be done with it. There was no satisfying closure. Lloyd's perversion was a heavy, stinking blanket they carried around that no one spoke of and that all of Barbara and Lloyd's friends pretended didn't exist. But little reminders of "the problem" cropped up regularly enough to destroy Molly's vision of life as good and luscious and far too short.

One evening, when Steve was at the hospital, Molly went into the boys' bedroom to tuck them into bed and have prayers with them as she always did. Jerry was already asleep in the bottom bunk; Teddy, however, was waiting for her with his chin in his hand, elbow bent. Molly made him relax his head on his pillow. Then she scratched his back and sang to him, had a short prayer, and told him good night.

But Teddy wasn't ready to go to sleep yet. Molly could tell that something was on his mind. She had had a call from his teacher that afternoon about some mischief he had been in at school, and she supposed he wanted to talk about that. Instead, he asked, "Mommy, am I gay?"

The question was so startling, it took Molly's breath away. Not till later would she know it was a question that held great significance. With some difficulty, Molly tried not to show her surprise—thinking that some of the talk-show or tabloid topics Teddy couldn't help but be aware of had confused him. She forced herself to hide her surprise. "Gay?" she asked lightly. "Why would you think you were gay, honey?"

"Well, Grandpa is, isn't he?" Teddy paused for her to answer. When she didn't speak, he raced on. "My best friends are boys, and I think girls are yuck. And I just wondered if that means I might be gay."

"Oh, honey." Molly brushed his hair back from his forehead, searching desperately for the right words to reassure him. "You're not gay. And Grandpa's not necessarily gay—he just was too friendly with kids—boys *and* girls. It's normal for nine- and ten-year-old boys to have best buddies who are boys. You're not gay."

"Well, do you think I'll turn gay when I get older?"

"Oh, no, honey. Why should you?"

His thin shoulders shrugged. "I dunno. Someone said you get it from your father."

"Your father's not gay, honey, so you don't have to worry."

"Yeah." A slow smile slid across his face. "I guess I'm OK."

"I'm not worried that you're gay," Molly said, giving him a kiss. "You're a normal, wonderful little boy. Now you go to sleep and don't think about it again."

"I will. But . . . Mommy? What exactly did Grandpa do to the kids?"

Molly let out a deep breath. "I don't know, honey. No one's ever told me."

"Then how did you know he did something bad?" He became defensive, sitting up in bed, his arms crossed on his chest. "You just don't like Grandpa, do you? You just want to make me not like Grandpa B because you think I like him more than I like Grandpa Spencer. You don't want me to like him, do you? That's why we didn't get to go to his house at Christmas this time, isn't it?" Teddy was pouting, his little chin pointing up defiantly.

"No, honey, that's not it," Molly said gently, her mind racing, choosing and discarding words frantically. She had to be so careful. "What Grandma Feldman told me is true; Grandma Bowker said it was too. Your grandpa has hurt some kids in the past. No one has told me exactly what he did, but it did happen. And Grandma Feldman said that if I didn't protect you, he might hurt you too. I didn't *want* to find out what he did to little boys. We're lucky we don't know. He didn't hurt you, honey, because I protected you—thanks to Grandma Feldman's warning."

"Did he hurt Daddy?"

Molly didn't want to answer. "We don't know, exactly," she said honestly.

Teddy thumped his crossed arms against his chest. "Well, I love him anyway. And he loves me. And you're not going to change that."

Molly prayed for wisdom. How could she make this child understand that she wasn't trying to build a wall between him and his grandpa? Why did Lloyd always come off being the "victim" and everyone else the persecutors? Finally, she said, "Honey, it's good that you love Grandpa. And I'm sure Grandpa loves you—in his own way." She had to add that. "But in a way he has hurt you already, hasn't he? He has made you think you might be gay, and he has made you feel unsafe at his house."

"Yeah. Once when I was taking my shower before bed, he came in the bathroom and pulled back the curtain and looked at me and said, 'Remember to wash your seat!' "

Molly was surprised. Teddy hadn't told her this before.

"Didn't you lock the door?"

"Oh, yes! I did! I always lock the door. He knocked on it, and I said the bathroom was busy. And then I heard him doing something to the doorknob, and he came in holding a screwdriver, and he looked at me and said to wash my seat. He asked if I needed any help, but I said No."

"You don't need any help with your bath," Molly agreed.

"Even Daddy doesn't wash me anymore. And when he did, he always used a washcloth—not his hand. Grandpa didn't have a washcloth with him."

This revelation made Molly's heart lurch about. What a cunning fox Lloyd had been. As closely as she had tried to guard her boys, Lloyd had thought up devious ways to get past her. He had almost gotten his hands on them. But—she sighed, feeling lucky—he had been foiled each time. Was it because, having been warned, the boys were aware of the danger? She gave the credit for that to precious Grandma Feldman. Still, what he had done was considered molesting. Looking at someone's genitals was a form of abuse; even talking sexually to a child or showing a child pornographic pictures was sex abuse. Steve's counselor had told them that.

Trying to complete this conversation, Molly said, "Well, it turned out all right, didn't it?" Teddy nodded. After a few moments of silence, while Molly stroked his forehead, she said, "It's all over. It's better not to think about stuff like that just before we go to sleep, though, OK? It's time for you to go to bed. Good night, sweetie."

Having expressed himself, Teddy seemed ready to let go of his anger at Molly. Another kiss, a quick "good night," and he settled under the covers to go to sleep.

But Molly couldn't dismiss so easily the thoughts her conversation with Teddy had raised. Lately, it seemed, she struggled constantly to maintain a calm and cheerful demeanor with the children. In fact, she felt she had to supply all the cheerfulness in their home. The children needed it from her. And Steve's temperament was so fragile, Molly was not comfortable sharing her burdens with him for fear they would weigh so heavily on him that he would retreat back into his world of narcotics.

And there was another strain on Molly's relationship with Steve. The way he said her name when they were lying in bed in the dark made her cringe and shiver. He sounded just like Lloyd. How painfully ironic: Steve, who had grown up with this strange man, was now free to forget him, while Molly, who had innocently married into the maelstrom, was stuck with reminders of him forever as she saw Lloyd in Steve. The conflict was incredible! How could she respond to a husband who bore some of the same characteristics that so repulsed her in another man? Sometimes it was too much. Tonight the house was sadly silent, dark, and depressing as Molly dragged herself down the creaking hall to the living room, clutching her Bible. She had always loved the Lord and had enjoyed teaching a children's class at every church they had attended since she was in college. Until recently, however, reading the Bible on her own hadn't meant much to her—she had always needed some sort of study guide. Now, as she forced herself to find something to be thankful for, it occurred to her that she had become more spiritual. Lately, she had begun searching the Scriptures for answers to questions that really meant something to her—answers that nobody gave in church.

"Of course no one gives me answers in church," she muttered to herself, recalling the secrecy with which Lloyd had left his teaching job thirty-eight years earlier. "Church members protect child molesters." Lloyd's molestations must have been fairly common knowledge among the school faculty and even in the local church if her roommate Leona's family had known about them. Why hadn't the church really dealt with the problem at that time, making Lloyd suffer the serious consequences he deserved? Why had they dropped the ball, allowing rumor to cloak the story in the guise of hurtful gossip, which made the hearers jump to Lloyd's defense?

Immediately, she felt guilty for her bitterness. But the questions refused to be pushed away. How could a church shield Lloyd when they knew what he'd done? How could they continue to let him hold church office? Why didn't someone come out and tell the truth?

The old clichéd answers came back to her. "Love your enemies," the preachers always said. Forgive "seventy times seven."

Really? Did these lines apply to active child molesters? The old familiar rhetoric that she was sure was meant to be comforting was, instead, building a wall between her and the church; had even strained her relationship with God.

When she had seen a counselor for some help on dealing with Steve and his family, the counselor had said, "You have been hurt badly, and you didn't deserve it." The counselor's support meant everything to her. Could she find that kind of support from the Bible?

Hearing nothing from the pulpit that made her feel better, Molly claimed the promise in Hebrews 11:6 that "God . . .

rewards those who earnestly seek him." She searched the Scriptures prayerfully, asking God to speak personally to her. She wanted to find that God hated Lloyd's sin as much she did; that He didn't walk the line, changing His tune to fit the occasion. She wanted to read from the Scriptures that a child molester's deeds were not just "little mistakes"—that they were grave mistakes, crimes.

The plump and time-worn sofa opened its arms to her, and she crawled into it as if it were her mother's lap. She curled her feet under her robe, switched on the crystal table lamp beside her, and opened the covers of her Bible. She had grown to love the crispy crinkle of the onion-skin paper. It brought back memories of family worships when she was a child. Each evening her father had selected just the right verses to read.

Where was that chapter in Luke her eyes had traveled to last week in church? Somewhere around the seventeenth chapter. She turned the thin pages carefully until she found the place, and then tenderly stroked them so they laid flat. This was it. Luke 17:1, 2: "Jesus said to his disciples: 'Things that cause people to sin are bound to come, but woe to that person through whom they come. It would be better for him to be thrown into the sea with a millstone tied around his neck than for him to cause *one of these little ones to sin*'" (italics supplied).

She could imagine a serious, no-nonsense look on Jesus' face and hear the between-the-lines message that said, "I am angry when people hurt children and separate them from Me. People who do that would be better off dead." Molly's eyes squeezed tightly together as hot, burning tears forced their way out. "Thank You, God," she whispered. "You *are* on Teddy's side."

Molly was certain God was speaking to her—not in a voice that anyone else could hear, but by impressions and insights. She closed her Bible with a sigh, then reopened it to Psalm 34:16: "The face of the Lord is against those who do evil, to cut off the memory of them from the earth." Her eyes wandered down to verse 18, and silent tears slipped down her cheeks as she read, "The Lord is close to the brokenhearted and saves those who are crushed in spirit. A righteous man may have many troubles, but the Lord delivers him from them all."

Molly laid her Bible on the table, wrapped her arms around her knees, and sobbed quietly for a while. Her tears seemed heavy, and her forehead sank to her knees. Suddenly, a feeling of total emptiness swept over her. Life seemed much too long.

"Help me, God," she whispered. "Help me get through this . . . please. And thank You for Your love . . . and Your justice."

Ah, justice. It was not what they preached from the pulpit, but it was everywhere in the Bible. Molly's God was not only a God of love, He was a God of justice as well. Sin—especially the sin that hurt children—angered Him.

Molly sat unmoving long after her tears were spent—until the mahogany clock on the mantel chimed nine. Glancing over at it, she seemed to come to life at last. Like an old woman, she collected herself and shuffled down the hall toward her bed. She would be asleep before Steve got home. He would never know how raw her feelings had been tonight.

CHAPTER
11

December 1980

Molly felt guilty about keeping the children from the Bowkers. She missed Barbara and knew that Barbara missed her grandchildren. Molly felt that now it would be safe to visit the Bowkers again because the boys, at eight and ten, were old enough to protect themselves from Lloyd. So, after a lonely Thanksgiving, she suggested to Steve, "Why don't we spend Christmas with your folks this year?"

"Are you sure?" Steve asked warily.

Molly nodded. "I miss your mom."

"Yeah, I guess so," Steve agreed. "All right. I'll call them and say we're coming."

It was, for the most part, a remarkably uneventful Christmas. Molly and Steve were the only ones sharing Christmas with the Bowkers that year, and Barbara and Lloyd showered the boys with toys. The boys most enjoyed the new pogo sticks they found under the tree on Christmas morning; they spent most of the day learning to balance on them. Molly and Steve even took their turns on the sticks, surprising the boys with their prowess. It was a wonderful, family-oriented Christmas Day.

The night before they were to leave, the air was frosty and still outside. Barbara made some popcorn while Lloyd stirred up the coals in the fireplace and laid large logs on them that soon were snapping and crackling cozily, sending up small explosions of brilliant orange sparks. Molly had mixed some punch and passed it around, and now she and Steve sat cuddled up on the couch, watching a special Christmas program on TV with the boys.

It had been exactly the kind of Christmas Molly had hoped it would be. She smiled a satisfied smile as Barbara came into the room with bowls of fragrant popcorn, took her place in her usual chair, and picked up her knitting.

When the program was over, a quiet peace settled over the family group. The fire had burned itself down again. Lloyd went out to his radio room, and Barbara busied herself in the kitchen. Molly and Steve pulled out the boys' sleeping bags and laid them in front of the fire.

"Go get your jammies on now, boys, and brush your teeth. It's time you were in bed," Molly said in warm tones. It felt so good to be happy.

With the boys settled for the night, Molly and Steve switched off the lights and, yawning, made their way down the hall to Patti's old room, where they always stayed. The bed had on it the same pink bedspread that Molly had laid Teddy on as a newborn; portraits of "Pinky" and "Blueboy" hung on the wall, and assorted crocheted doilies that Barbara had made through the years adorned the dresser and hope chest in the room.

Stepping out of her soft pink bathrobe and slipping her legs between the sheets, Molly shivered a little at the cold. "I hope the boys will be warm enough," she worried.

"Oh, yeah. They're OK. They're in front of the fire," Steve said. "What's the matter? Don't you like cold sheets?"

"No, as a matter of fact—I don't. Get in here and warm them up for me!"

They read in companionable silence for some time. Then Steve turned out the light, and they settled themselves for sleep. The distant, crashing surf provided a hypnotic background to the snapping of ice crystals on the trees as Molly felt herself drifting off slowly to a wonderful sleep.

She was awakened shortly by a warm hand on her arm.

"Mommy! Mommy!"

Instinctively, Molly put out her hand and shoved away the intrusion. Then she wearily opened her eyes. Eight-year-old Jerry was standing at her bedside—bereft of pajamas, wearing only his underwear.

"Mommy, Grandpa's put too many logs on the fire, and Teddy

and I are too hot. Grandpa's giving us backrubs, and we can't go to sleep."

"What?" At the mention of backrubs, Steve was alert.

"Your dad's got the fire too hot for the boys," Molly said. She tensed, and her mind began racing as she stepped into her bathrobe.

"I'll go," Steve said firmly.

"I'm coming too," Molly told him. She hoped that Lloyd had innocently been trying to help, but her intuition told her otherwise. How dare he ruin what, till now, had been a wonderful Christmas?

The living room was so hot, Molly was surprised the woodwork wasn't glowing. Teddy sat on his sleeping bag in his underwear, fanning his face, staring at the fire. Lloyd's silhouette loomed large and frightening in front of the roaring orange flames.

"What are you doing here?" Steve demanded of Lloyd.

"This is my house," Lloyd returned defensively, his voice reedy. "I live here."

Jerry said, "Grandpa was going to give us a backrub. But he made it too hot. We had to take our jammies off."

"Well, I didn't want you to get too cold," Lloyd explained lamely, in a voice frighteningly sugarcoated, yet quavering like a child's who knows he has been caught doing wrong.

"You had no right to wake them up," Molly said. "I had already put them to sleep. The fire was perfect. They didn't need backrubs." She went to the front door and opened it, swinging it back and forth like a fan to bring in some cool air. The mood in the room made her shiver despite the heat. "What exactly were you trying to do?" Molly demanded to know.

Steve grabbed a piece of wood near the fireplace and spread the logs apart so the fire would die down. "This is insane," he said. "Where are the fireplace tools?"

When Steve and Molly had first come into the living room, Lloyd had begun pacing like a lion. At Steve's question, he slammed out the kitchen door and disappeared into the garage. But no sooner had Molly sighed in relief than he returned with a pair of fireplace tongs and forced his way past Steve to the fire.

Molly watched in horrified silence as Lloyd lifted a burning log from the fire and carried it over the boys' heads, dropping burning embers onto their legs, their sleeping bags, and the carpet. The boys shrieked, "Grandpa! Watch out!" and began hitting at the sparks with their bare hands.

"What are you doing?" Molly shouted.

But, like a crazed man, Lloyd was deaf to their cries. Without answering, he brushed past Molly and threw the burning log into the yard. Then he returned to repeat the dangerous trek as the boys shrieked in fright once more and scrambled on hands and knees to get out of the way.

"What are you doing?" Molly shouted again as he passed her. She grabbed his arm and shook it, surprised at her own strength.

Lloyd stopped in front of her with the glowing log and glared at her. He wrenched his arm away from her, and the evil in his eyes made her drop her gaze. Lloyd turned to face Steve. "You always want to be in control!" he shouted across the room.

Molly's heart was hammering so hard, she thought her head was going to explode. She tasted bile. Never before had she felt such evil; it was like a dark, foreboding presence.

Lloyd dropped the second log onto the frozen grass and continued around the outside of the house to the garage.

When the temperature in the room had dropped to a comfortable level again, Molly shut the door and knelt with Steve to gather the boys in their arms.

"What was the matter with Grandpa?" Jerry asked.

"I don't know, honey," Molly told him.

He said in a small voice, "I'm scared. I want to sleep in your room."

"Me too," Teddy echoed.

"OK," Molly agreed. They dragged the sleeping bags down the hall and spread them out in the cramped walking space on either side of the bed. Once more they settled down for sleep—but this time Molly's thoughts were churning. What was Lloyd really trying to do? Where was Barbara during all this? Was it possible that Jerry had averted the unspeakable by waking her up? She scolded herself for thinking the worst of Lloyd. Surely it was all a gross misunderstanding. Still, Molly was glad they were going home in the morning.

CHAPTER

12

September 1983

One day at a time. One day at a time. Molly found herself needing to repeat that phrase to herself regularly. Steve continued to attend group therapy off and on at a drug-dependency clinic—mostly after a crisis, when Molly discovered and confronted him with a forgotten vial of Demerol hidden between the waterbed frame and the mattress or taped to the underside of a drawer, or when fresh bloodstains on the sheets evidenced a recent injection. Chagrined, Steve found a group therapy session in town that was geared specifically for spouses of drug abusers and asked Molly to attend with him. Molly agreed reluctantly.

The group was a rough bunch. The first time she sat in the circle with unshaven, bare-chested heroin addicts who wore leather vests, dirty red bandannas tied tightly around their heads, and four earrings dangling from each ear, Molly shivered. As they went around the circle and confessed their heroin addictions, it was apparent that Steve's addiction was a much different kind of problem than theirs.

But everyone seemed polite enough that first night. As the hour rushed by, Molly began to enjoy expressing her feelings—until one of the two counselors stood behind Steve to speak for him in a role-playing situation. The counselor explained that their purpose was to help Steve by putting into words what he might wish he could say when Molly asked him why he had let her down.

"I don't see why you had to get addicted to drugs," Molly said to Steve. "Why can't you just take them the way they're supposed to be taken—only when you need them and in the usual doses? Why are you so sneaky about it?"

The counselor's reply was very smooth. He had an answer to each of Molly's questions. "I wouldn't have to sneak if you would just accept me the way I am," he said confrontationally.

"But I can't accept your taking drugs," Molly replied, "because I care about you. You don't need them anymore; it's been years since your surgeries. They're only harming you now."

"You have no idea what it's like to be hurting, do you?" the counselor answered vehemently. "You with your perfect family and your loving mother and father. You'll never understand what I've been through."

"And you can't understand the pain you've brought to *me*," Molly said past a lump that was beginning to form in her throat.

"My pain is bigger," the counselor said.

Molly sought understanding, but the counselor was not going to give it to her. Molly felt that he was baiting her. The agonizing five minutes that the banter went on seemed like hours. Steve kept his eyes on the floor. Finally, feeling helpless, Molly began to cry. She wanted out of this role-playing situation. "Why doesn't anyone help me? Why am I expected to always be the strong one?" She looked toward the other counselor. "Why don't you stand behind *me*?" she pleaded. "Why is everyone on his side?"

The counselor behind Steve, still speaking for him, said, "Don't turn on the tears now. I'm the one who should be crying."

Molly shook her head. "I'm not doing this," she said flatly. "This isn't fair." She reached down beside her chair for her purse and fumbled for a tissue.

Finally, the counselor stepped out from behind Steve and took his chair. "Perhaps now you can see what Steve may be thinking when you keep asking him why he's using drugs. He may not really know!"

Molly blew her nose and dabbed at her eyes, but nobody seemed to notice that she was in pain.

Another couple did some role-playing of the same kind. Molly remained stiffly in her seat throughout the rest of the meeting, feeling desperately uncomfortable, unsafe. Finally the session was over. Molly didn't want to ever come back, and she told the counselor so.

"It's really best if you come together," he insisted, "if you really do want to help Steve." So the next week they met there again after work, coming in separate cars. The discussion came around to commitment to a marriage partner. Molly spoke up almost without thinking. "How can you sleep with someone else, knowing the pain you will bring to your partner?"

"It happens," one of the crustier males spoke up, shrugging his shoulders, leaning his chair back on two legs, and holding his hands up in the air. "Hey. It just happens. Might even happen to you someday, you little Christian." His top lip curled in a frightening sneer that showed missing teeth.

"No," Molly said firmly with a shake of her head, surprised at the strength of her answer. She forced a smile to soften the abruptness. "I'll never commit adultery."

"Now, now, not so fast, your holiness." The front legs of the chair returned to the floor with a thud. "You're a pretty self-assured Christian," he sneered. "But I've read your little Bible before. Doesn't it say 'let him who thinks he stands take heed lest he falls'?"

Molly nodded. "And I *might* fall in many other ways; I'm not perfect. But I just know that having an affair is not one of my weak points. I just won't let it happen."

"Oh, pretty words," he said, his mouth turned down tightly against his rotting teeth. The others joined in, taunting her. Everyone was talking at once, jabbing their fingers at her and rolling their eyes at the ceiling, shouting obscenities.

It was several minutes before the counselors regained control of the group. Molly was near tears, her heart pounding in her head. What was so wrong about knowing where your strengths were? In one agonizing moment she hated Steve; hated him for having a perverted father; hated him for escaping into his drugged stupors and not being a companion for her. Most of all, she hated him for bringing her to this nightmare—this darkly paneled, messy room that smelled of old coffee and cigarettes, where these people out of her worst nightmares threatened her.

Looking around the room at their rotting teeth and their sweaty bodies, she wished it were a dream instead of reality. She was trapped here with them because of what her husband had done. But she and Steve weren't of the same caliber as these people! Steve was a doctor. Dr. and Mrs. Bowker didn't belong here!

Molly thought she was going to vomit. Never before had she felt so claustrophobic, so out of place. She would not stay. She couldn't. Bolting noisily from her chair, she ran to the narrow wooden stairway. The pounding roar of her feet on the stairs filled her head as she hurried toward the exit door, both hands slamming against the smooth, cool surface of the glass as she ran outside like one pursued by the devil himself. She stood at last beside the car, her sides heaving, head resting on the hood, crying like a baby and spitting bitter vomit onto the gravel between her feet.

"Molly!" Steve had followed her anxiously. "I'm sorry, Molly. Are you OK?"

She couldn't speak, her body was so racked by great, gasping sobs.

"Molly, I'm so sorry I got you into this mess." He sounded truly contrite, near tears. "What's happening to us?"

"That's what I'd like to know." She had found her voice, but it was not stern. Rather, she spoke listlessly, like a little girl, drained as she was of every ounce of energy. "I think I'm going to die," she said, looking up at him helplessly with a crumpled face she could not control. "I'm not going to make it till you're well, Steve. It's taking too long." She pressed her fingers to her lips, her eyes stinging, as though that would stop the tears. But it didn't.

Wordlessly, Steve pulled her to him and folded her in his arms. She could hear the strong and steady heartbeat that used to reassure her, and she smelled again the lemony fragrance of his cologne. It had been a long time since he had held her like this. She began to relax, feeling better, but knowing the peace would not last. Something else would come up to worry her. It always did—always had for the entire fifteen years of their married life. This was not the future she had imagined for herself as a little girl. This was not even a nightmare she had had—

it was much, much more horrifying than she could have ever imagined. She had met this man in a Christian college, and yet the life they had made together was one of dark secrets and ugly perversion and drug therapy with immoral heroin addicts who despised her Christianity.

"I'm sorry I've hurt you, Molly," Steve began, his cheek pressed against the top of her head. "I don't know why I'm doing this; why I can't stop. Sometimes I think how easy it would be just to not make the corner over the bridge on my way home and get out of your life."

"Oh, Steve, don't. Don't talk that way."

"No, it's true. I've been nothing but trouble for you, and you deserve better than that. It would be better for you if I just got out of your life and you could find someone else."

Molly shook her head. "If you want out of my life, there are other, less dramatic ways to do it. The boys would be devastated if you killed yourself."

"They wouldn't know it was a suicide."

"It would still hurt them. Don't talk that way, Steve. I don't have the strength to be your counselor right now. Just do something for me, OK?"

"Anything."

"Promise me you won't pull any surprises like that—that driving off a bridge—so I don't have to worry if you're late coming home. I can't take any more stress right now."

"OK. But the pressure is killing me, Molly. I'm around drugs all day long. I order them for my patients. Do you know how hard it is for me?"

"I'm sure it is. But don't think of it as a temptation; think of it as a way to make you stronger."

"But it hasn't. Can't you see? That's why I'm in this mess. I think about them all day long; I have friends who can order them for me—" He released her and rested a hand on the hood of the car, looked away, and ran the fingers of his other hand through his hair. "I didn't want to tell you this tonight—" He looked up at the stars and then down at his feet. "I've decided to drop out of my residency until I beat this thing with the Demerol. I can't be ordering drugs for people when I have a problem with them myself. A doped-up doctor isn't safe."

Molly's mouth dropped open. "What are you going to do?" She brushed roughly at the tears on her cheeks.

Steve shoved his hands deep into his trouser pockets, shook his head, and opened and then shut his mouth without saying anything. At last he found his voice. "Well," he said, speaking more slowly than usual. "If there's one good thing my father did for me, he gave me experience as a landscaper. I know I can get a job with just about any landscaping company. We can move back to Seattle—you liked it there. I can landscape for a while. I can always teach or something in the future, so my medical school isn't a total waste."

"Oh, Steve." Molly leaned back against the car dejectedly as a bone-chilling weariness crept over her. "When is it all going to stop?"

"My father always said I'd never amount to anything," Steve answered dejectedly. "I guess he was right."

Molly shook her head weakly. "Don't say that. Don't give him that power over you. Just because you don't work as a doctor doesn't mean you're not worth anything." She sighed. "I'm so tired of this."

"Why don't you just hit me?" The words came out of Steve's mouth without emotion, and Molly stared at him in utter disbelief.

"And what good would it do to hit you?" she asked.

"You deserve to hit me," he said in a flat voice.

Molly shook her head. "Don't do this, Steve. When has hitting ever solved anything?"

She turned her back to him, got into her car, and started home. But her mind wasn't on her driving, and she accidentally took a wrong turn off the freeway and found herself in a strange part of town. It seemed natural—everything else was going so wrong! Now she was lost late at night on a strange street where anything might happen and she knew nobody at all. For one painful moment, she wished a stray bullet *would* find her. Death was the ultimate problem solver—for the dead person.

Her face and eyes throbbed from crying. They ached so badly that she didn't want to talk to anyone. But finally she admitted to herself that she couldn't find her way back home, and she must keep on keeping on—for the children. Ironically, the anxiety of being lost was nothing compared to the sense of doom she felt when she thought about where Steve's addiction was taking her.

She stopped at a filling station and asked for directions back onto the freeway. Once back on the familiar road, the numbness that was also familiar came over her, and she drove like a robot toward home.

To her surprise, Steve was waiting up for her. "I was worried about you," he said.

"If you were really worried, you wouldn't do what you do," she heard herself saying in a flat voice. "I'm not going back to that counseling center ever again. I was verbally abused tonight, and I won't let it happen again."

Steve apologized as though he were responsible and said he wouldn't return either. Molly didn't have the strength to encourage him to go. She accepted his apology in silence and prepared herself for a troubled sleep.

The next morning Molly called her mother in Michigan. "Hi, Mom. What's going on?" she asked blandly, trying to borrow some happiness.

"Oh, Linda and Kevin are here with the kids, and we're having a corn roast. Wish you were here too."

"I'm glad someone's having fun," Molly said quietly.

Kate guessed immediately that something was wrong. "What's happened, honey?" she asked gently.

"Steve's quit his residency till he gets off the Demerol—maybe forever. I don't know how to help him," Molly said tearfully.

"Well, you can't, honey," her mother replied. "It has to be his choice."

"I know. But the waiting is killing me. I don't know why he can't stop. I'll think he's over it, and then he's conked out again and has that bright look in his eyes when I wake him up. Or I'll find a bottle of Demerol in the glove box or even on the seat. He dumps it down the toilet in a grand show of quitting, but then I'll find some more again later. It's not ending, Mom. And I don't know what to do! I'm being eaten alive inside! I've told

God that I'm willing to die if that's what it would take to shake Steve up. Each time I get into the car, I confess my sins so that I'm ready for death. But the pressure is killing me, Mom." Molly broke into a sob.

"I'm sure it's tough, honey. But God's not going to kill you. You can help Steve in other ways. If you need to get away for a while, you can always bring the boys and spend some time with us."

"I know, and thanks." Molly sniffed, struggling to regain her composure. "I'll be OK. I just had to tell someone. I think we're moving back to Seattle. We've got friends there, and maybe Steve can teach at the university someday. They liked him when he was a student."

"Uh-huh," Kate said. "I'm sorry, honey. I feel partly responsible for all your problems."

"Why?"

"Well, Daddy and I should have talked to you more before you married. We had some concerns. You didn't know Steve very well, and—"

"Mom, you aren't responsible for any of this," Molly assured her. "If you had told me I couldn't marry Steve, I probably would have been even more loyal to him—you know how love-struck teenagers are. I had concerns, too, but I was naive and thought that just because *your* marriage was happy, mine would automatically be happy too. I thought I could help him. I made my bed; I can sleep in it. Please don't hold yourself responsible. I'm a big girl; I'll make it through this all right."

As Molly hung up the phone, she realized despairingly that she was emotionally numb. She trembled as she remembered the events of the night before, but now she felt neither anger nor fear, just a cold emptiness. She went about her daily tasks as though in a daze, finding it hard to concentrate, feeling nothing toward Steve and nothing for her boys, around whom her life had once been centered. That surprised her the most. At one time, her biggest ambition in life had been to get married and be a mommy. Now Molly didn't even feel like being a mommy anymore. She answered the questions the boys asked and sent them off to school with a smile—but she knew that the smile was merely painted on her face. It didn't come from deep inside as it once had. How long would this numbness continue? She was beginning to feel desperate. She found herself wishing she were a nun.

She realized that she was beginning to remind herself of the psychiatric patients she had seen in the wards during her psych rotation, and the realization frightened her. She pulled her psychology book from the bookcase and leafed through it. In the chapter on stress, the author had written: "Stress can be caused by feeling helpless and at the mercy of others. Patients need to feel they have some measure of control in order to lessen their stress and anxiety levels."

That made sense. She was feeling out of control—like a person at the end of the line when they played Crack the Whip on rollerskates at school. The person at the end of the whip went careening around the gym floor—unless he let go. If he let go, he could stop—though not without a struggle. But he could always let go. She could let go too . . . of Steve. Even let go of his name. She had a choice. There were other roller coasters she could ride as a single parent if she didn't like this one that Steve was taking her on—this emotional roller coaster of mistrust—of not knowing what he was going to do next to cause her anxiety.

Somehow, just knowing she had the choice of leaving or staying made her feel better. But she didn't want to leave. Too many of her childhood dreams about marriage had already been shattered. Choosing divorce would just add another shattered dream to that list. And so she chose to stay. She also chose to grant herself the freedom to reexamine that decision at any time, determining not to sacrifice her health for the sake of staying married. She and Barbara were similar in many ways. But unlike Barbara, Molly would not stay with a man who abused her. Molly had sometimes felt pity for Barbara, but now she regarded her with more frustration than pity. Why hadn't she said something about Lloyd to someone years before? More importantly, why had she gone ahead with her wedding after Lloyd was fired for his "indiscretions"?

Before she sat down to fold the laundry, Molly put a tape of religious songs in the stereo and turned the volume up so the words and music embraced her with their warm message of hope. The song spoke to her of how Jesus could turn her sorrow into joy if she turned her shattered life over to Him. As she listened, Molly deliberately forced herself tocry till the pressures inside her released and the tears became real. She pleaded with God to bring her some joy—to use this experience for some good.

Molly and Steve packed up their things and moved to Ballard, Washington, into a rental house owned by the parents of one of their friends. It was an old Victorian house with a large front porch; spreading maple trees lined the sidewalk in front. Steve soon lined up a job with a landscaping company, and Molly found work at a hospital downtown.

Forcing herself to look ahead and not back, Molly felt a surprising sense of delightful anticipation about the future. She had somehow found the strength to make an appointment with a marriage counselor, and she and Steve had begun therapy—which gave Molly another fresh-start honeymoon period with both Steve and the boys. With this renewed move toward normalcy in their family, Molly suggested that they spend Christmas with Barbara and Lloyd, Patti and the twins, and their families. They hadn't been "back home" for two years.

Molly was eager to visit with Chad and Paige and their three-year-old daughter, Megan. Paige had been good about sending pictures, so Molly knew that Megan was a darling with a round, cherubic face and a cap of soft blond curls. Molly's own boys were growing out of childhood into adolescence. Teddy was thirteen and Jerry had just turned eleven, so Molly felt a longing to hold a little someone on her lap and read stories to her and receive sweet kisses like she did when her boys were three.

They arrived on Christmas Eve. Barbara greeted them with her traditional apron tied around her waist, and Lloyd good-naturedly helped remove the suitcases from the car, giving the boys a friendly wallop on their backsides as a greeting. He and Steve shook hands, though Barbara reached high and threw her dimpled, doughy arms around her oldest son's neck and hugged him tightly. "Ummm. So good to see you!" she said. Her voice was warm. Molly was taken into her ample bosom just as warmly.

Megan was as sweet as she had seemed in her pictures. After

giving her Aunt Molly a quick kiss, she brought over her newest dolly. "Shall I sit on your lap?" she suggested with a light and bubbly laugh, and then proceeded to tell Molly where to sit and how far back in the chair and how to lift her up just right. Before the weekend was three hours old, Megan and Molly were practically inseparable.

"Where are you sleeping tonight?" Megan's baby voice floated over the sound of the other voices.

Molly replied, "I think Uncle Steve and I are sleeping in the family room. Where are you sleeping?"

"I'm staying in my daddy's room! I'm ... I'm staying in my daddy's room where he was just a little boy ... but now he's a BIG boy." She stretched out the word *big*, and her eyes grew round and long to match her oval mouth. And after she said it, she giggled and slapped her hands to her mouth and threw her arms around Molly's neck in an impulsive hug.

Barbara had loaded a lace-covered snack table with cheese balls and crackers on her best china platters, caramel-coated nuts in footed silver dishes, and finger sandwiches of egg salad and cheese on white bread with the crusts carefully trimmed. A punch bowl of tangy cranberry juice in which mint leaves were floating graced the center of the table. As everyone filled their plates, Lloyd came and stood beside Paige. Molly couldn't help but notice that since Paige had joined the family, Lloyd had been pushing himself onto her instead of Molly.

Now Lloyd was talking about someone at church who was divorced and who had so appreciated the wood he had cut for her. "She's got the cutest little kids! The little boy, who's about six, was climbing all over my lap in the truck and hanging onto my leg as I walked. He wanted to see my truck. So when I was all done with the wood I took him inside the truck and showed him all the shelves and my tools and gave him a petunia plant left over from the last job I did. He was jumping up and down, and the doors closed on us, and the poor fella started screaming and crying because it was so dark."

Lloyd chuckled, remembering. Barbara's shoulders went up to her ears, and she chuckled too.

Molly said, "Oh, poor little boy."

Lloyd waved off the comment with a shrug. "He was OK. As soon as I opened the doors, he hopped out and ran to his mother. I explained the whole thing, and she understood. She wasn't mad—how could she be, after I'd just split and stacked all that firewood?"

Lloyd laughed again and then stuffed his mouth with a cracker that bore a glob dug from the smoke-flavored cheese ball. Molly wondered what details Lloyd was leaving out of the story, but silently chided herself for thinking the worst.

Soon, Lloyd brought out his Bible and read the Christmas story from the book of Luke, stopping abruptly and staring icily into the Bible for several agonizing seconds when anyone moved or coughed. Then, after his customary long prayer, he took his place under the tree as the official gift distributor. Teddy asked if he could help pass out the presents. When Lloyd pretended not to hear, Molly realized he was getting into one of his dominant moods. Hiding her impatience, she leaned forward and said with a smile, "Lloyd? Teddy's trying to ask you something."

Lloyd did not return her smile. Taking a moment to stop sorting through the packages, he looked at Molly briefly. "I know. I don't need any help."

Teddy, sitting near the tree, looked uncomfortable. Then he leaned forward to straighten the tag on one of the presents. "Hey. This is mine!" he whooped happily. "I want this one first, Grandpa." Teddy's face was shining expectantly.

Lloyd was instantly alert. Snatching the present from the startled teen, he bellowed. "Hey! That's my job. You'll get your present when I say so."

Molly could tell by the way her son's eyes groped for the ceiling that he was near tears. The Christmas atmosphere shattered, she wanted to get up and leave. But she forced herself to stay—hoping the evening would improve once the ritual started.

Lloyd found a present for each of the grown-ups and then for each of the grandchildren, making Teddy wait till last because he had been so forward as to make a request. The sparkling jumble of goodies under the tree still had hardly a dent in it when Lloyd started making the rounds again.

Teddy and Jerry had made a gift for their father, and Molly

crawled over to point it out and whisper to Lloyd that the boys wanted to give it to their father themselves. No sooner had she done so than Lloyd picked up the package and ceremoniously placed it in Steve's lap himself.

The boys looked at their mother with crestfallen faces. Seeing their hurt, she said quickly, "Oh, Steve? The boys wanted to give that to you themselves. Go ahead, boys. Steve, if you'll hand it to them, they can give it back to you." It was a stupid attempt at correcting Lloyd's action. She knew it but couldn't stop herself.

"That's OK," Teddy said, and Jerry nodded regretfully.

"Oops!" Lloyd said. "That's the one you just told me about, isn't it? Bub-bub-bub-bub." Like a gradeschooler, he flicked his bottom lip with two of his fingers to make the sound.

Molly swallowed the rage that was burning deep inside, feeling the heat as though she were glowing. Lloyd was impossible to read. He could be so kind and sweet one moment and then turn into an arrogant, unfeeling snob within the time it took to take a breath. Being around him was like walking on eggshells. Sometimes he could be trusted, and sometimes he couldn't—which, in the long run, meant a person had to regard him as basically untrustworthy.

"Well, thank you, boys!" Steve said warmly. He pulled out a wooden rack onto which lids from baby food jars had been nailed, the empty jars screwed into the lids.

"You can keep seeds and stuff in them," Jerry explained proudly.

"It's really nice," Steve said, and he patted the boys' shoulders and then shook their hands.

Since Teddy had become a teenager, Steve had been increasingly uncomfortable with hugging the boys. When he was home to wish them good night, he never kissed them—just shook their hands. It bothered Molly, but fearing the argument it would cause if she brought it up, she hadn't said anything. But with their renewed attempts to establish open relationships in their family, she decided she would mention it soon.

At last the exhausting Christmas Eve was over. Megan was already asleep in her sleeping bag on the floor of her parents' room when Barbara bustled everyone else out of the living room. Then she and Lloyd cleaned up the wrapping-paper mess and stuffed and hung the stockings. Molly was grateful that Barbara had offered to take care of the stockings for all of them. After the stressful evening, she just wanted to go to sleep.

Molly awoke quite slowly. The refreshing sleep had put her in a good mood—better than she had known for a while. The sun was shining through the pale pink curtains, and Steve was there beside her. It was Christmas morning! Hearing muffled sounds out in the hall and the bubbling laughter of the children as they counted the goodies in their stockings, Molly rolled out of bed, pulled on her new white chenille robe, and ran her fingers through her auburn hair, which had grown quite long. Her fingers quickly wove her hair into a French braid to get it out of her face. It was good to feel happy again. With a smile glowing on her face, she padded toward the living room to watch the children.

As she passed Paige and Chad's bedroom, Paige opened the door and pulled her inside. "Megan's been molested," Paige hissed in a constricted voice. Her face was twisted like crumpled paper, and it was apparent she had been crying.

Molly's eyes took in the little girl sitting quietly on the bed in her flannel nightie, sucking on a lollypop, the goodies from her stocking spread all around her. She didn't want to believe it—didn't want to believe that Grandma and Grandpa's house was a dangerous trap.

"How do you know?" Molly asked, caressing the top of the little girl's head with her eyes.

"It happened early this morning." Covering her face in her hands, Paige lowered herself onto the bed, and Chad picked up the story.

"I've never trusted Dad, you know, after what he did to Cody. When I closed the door last night, I shoved our suitcases up against it so Megan couldn't get out without my knowing it and so I'd hear if he opened the door. But this morning the suitcases were moved, and Megan was gone. I found her in my parents' bed without her panties on."

Paige finished the story for him. "She's red and sore, and she screamed when she went potty."

Megan looked up at Molly. "My pee-pee hurts," she said, nodding.

Feeling lifeless, Molly sat down weakly, cradling her head in her hands and struggling to catch her breath. "Are you sure?" she managed to ask, hoping there had been some mistake. It was too much to take in. Molly had thought she saw a light at the end of the tunnel, but the light was a thundering train. Didn't it always happen like this? The moment she felt happy, something came along to take all that happiness away. She was beginning to fear happiness, thinking it only an illusion—an attempt to escape the truth that life cannot be happy. She wondered if those who appear happy are just playing a role. Perhaps, she thought, stress is the reality, and happiness is a mental illness that the unstable wear for protection. Then she wondered whether the horrible events that had filled her life since her marriage had made *her* mentally ill.

Paige shook her head in response to Molly's question. "I'm sure it happened. Just as sure as I was the weekend of my wedding when he molested Cody out in the field."

"He did?"

"Don't you remember that night? Cody came in crying—"

"Yes, I remember. But I hoped I was wrong."

"My mom finally got Cody to talk about it. Lloyd had molested him. But I never thought he'd do it to one of his own."

"Oh, Paige," Molly cried, and held out her hands to her sister-in-law. Then she said, "You need to report him."

"I don't think so."

"Why not?"

"Well . . ." Paige struggled for words. "We're not *absolutely* sure; it could be a misunderstanding."

Molly urged more strongly. "Please report him; he needs to experience a consequence for what he's been doing."

Paige squirmed uncomfortably. "I think it's best kept from the police. Perhaps counseling would help."

Molly understood. Megan was so young, and Chad and Paige probably worried that an interrogation by the police might be too frightening. At length, she asked, "Does Patti know?"

"Not yet."

"She needs to. I'll go get her." Molly found Patti in the kitchen, amiably helping her mother with brunch. "Could I steal her for a second?" she asked, and Barbara nodded.

Motioning for Patti to follow her, she said, "Get Roger, and I'll get Steve. We need to talk. I'll meet you in Paige and Chad's room."

Quietly, Chad and Paige repeated the story. Steve and Patti had a difficult time believing their father would do such a thing. "You'd believe it if it happened to your child," Chad said. "And what's really hard to believe is that it happened in their bed, and Mom was right there while it happened. She didn't protect my baby!"

They stood dumbstruck for several minutes. Then Molly asked softly, "What do we do now?"

"We can't stay," Paige said with a shake of her head.

Molly agreed. "I'm not comfortable, either."

"I can't leave," Patti said regretfully.

"Why not?" Steve challenged her.

"I don't know. It's just so hard to believe."

Steve shook his head, finding it difficult to understand his sister. Turning to Chad, he asked in a shaking voice, "And who is going to break the news to Mom and Dad?"

"I'll tell them we're leaving." Paige had a determined, no-nonsense look about her. "I've already talked to them this morning, and it can be just a continuation of that conversation. Lloyd stomped out to the radio room after I confronted him this morning, so I'll just tell Barbara, and then we can leave."

It was a subdued group that closed the suitcases and dragged them out to the cars, along with the piles of new toys the grandparents had given. Molly would have left the presents if her boys weren't so taken by them. She hated to leave Barbara. Barbara was so good with the children—so warm and interested, like a Norman Rockwell grandma would be. But along with Barbara came Lloyd and his malevolent perversion; the evil in the home was driving them from the good.

Molly knew their leaving was going to hurt Barbara, and

she hated Lloyd for that. Life was so unfair. This latest incident would hurt her children too. Lloyd and Barbara were the grandparents they had lived near enough to see regularly—and now she wouldn't ever feel safe visiting them. Her own parents, though also loving and warm, lived so far away they saw the children only once or twice a year and then only for short visits. Molly felt the burning again, deep in her gut. She was breathing fast and shallowly. Lloyd was taking so much away from so many for his own selfish reasons, and Barbara was allowing it.

The house smelled heavenly of fresh banana-nut muffins, the table was set with the Christmas china, Andy Williams was crooning Christmas music, and the Christmas tree blinked cheerfully—but most of the guests were leaving. Barbara hugged each of them for a long time, but she didn't shed a tear. Stoically, she gave each one a smile and wished them a safe drive home as she waved alone from the porch. To the neighbors, it must have appeared to be a normal leaving—a friendly farewell.

The crisp, winter air was clean, and Molly, trudging toward the car, took big lungfuls of it—anything to rid herself of the filth that had happened inside that house.

"Why are we leaving?" Jerry asked, and Molly shushed him. "Get in the car, and I'll tell you later," she said.

But he wasn't through talking. "Grandpa was just going to show me his computer stuff."

"Just get in the car," Molly said conspiratorially, out of the corner of her mouth. "I'll explain later."

The tires spun in the snow until Steve let up a little on the accelerator. Then the chains grabbed and melodically chinged along the road as they crept out of the neighborhood like naughty children. This was supposed to have been a loving Christmas. But Lloyd had done wrong, and in doing so, had forced his grown children to also do what seemed wrong—to leave a gracious hostess. But the safety of the children demanded it.

Still, Molly wondered whether they were doing the right thing. She shook her head as though to shake off the guilt and forced herself to admire the scenery outside: the pristine whiteness of the snow, piled like down on the towering pines—which stretched their branches out above the ground like women inspecting their just-polished fingernails. The sun shimmered on a thin crust of ice along the road, and Molly closed her eyes against the glare.

"Mommy?" It was Jerry, bringing her back to their conversation. "Why are we leaving?"

Molly struggled to find the appropriate words, then decided a direct explanation would work best. "Grandpa hurt Megan," she said, "and we felt it wasn't safe to stay."

"Well, he didn't hurt me."

"Not yet, anyway," Molly said gratefully.

"What exactly did he do?" Teddy asked.

Steve glanced at Molly. His knuckles were white on the steering wheel. Molly swallowed and said, "He touched her private parts."

They rode along in silence for several miles, each one absorbed in his own private misery. Then Jerry asked, "Are we ever going to see them again?"

"I don't know," Molly said. "Aunt Paige and Uncle Chad are going to talk to a counselor where they live and ask him for advice. Then we'll decide. Right now, I doubt that we'll ever see Grandpa and Grandma again."

Jerry nodded and turned his face back to the window. He busied himself blowing steam on the window and drawing pictures in it with his fingertip. Teddy had not said a word. He stared solemnly out the window, alone with his thoughts.

CHAPTER
13

1984

The new year, 1984, began in a blur. A doctor examined little Megan and confirmed her parents' suspicions. The doctor ordered all contact with Lloyd stopped. He said Lloyd must begin therapy, and added that as part of it, Lloyd would probably be required to pay for whatever therapy expenses his victims incurred. Chad and Paige struck up a deal of sorts—if Lloyd obtained therapy, they wouldn't report the molestation to the police.

At Molly's insistence, Steve also began therapy again—as a means of helping him remember whether he had been molested. They arranged for his counseling bills to be sent to Barbara, and she paid them. Surprisingly, Patti offered to tell Lloyd that none of the children would be seeing him until his counselor told them he was safe with children.

During all the confusion, a smoldering hatred had begun to show in Teddy. Molly didn't know why he had changed so much but chose to blame it on his adolescence—he turned fourteen in June. His patience was limited, and he often lashed out verbally at his brother. He was suspended from school on several occasions and used the free time to sleep for twelve to fourteen hours at a time. When he showered, it was always for far too long, and Steve would pound on the bathroom door to get him out. He began spitting on the ground whenever he was outside—not once or twice, but often.

One evening he came to the family room after another of his long showers and stood by the woodstove with his hands in front of him, enjoying the heat. Steve confronted him about the length of his shower. "Didn't you hear me pounding on the door?" he asked, obviously angry.

"Yeah, I did. But I wasn't finished."

"You've got to cut down on your showers, kid. I'm paying for each and every drop you waste. Do you want me to come in and turn off the water for you next time?"

Teddy reacted as if he'd seen a ghost. His eyes became round and suddenly fearful. His jaw began to tremble, and he drew his hands to his chest as if to protect himself. "Not you too," he said in a desperate, almost pleading voice. He was crying big tears, squeezing his eyes tightly together. His mouth opened silently like a fish out of water as he panted and wiped helplessly at the tears.

Steve didn't notice the effect his words were having on Teddy. But Molly leapt to her feet and put her arms around their son. "Oh, honey, if you're afraid that your dad's going to hurt you like Lloyd hurt Megan, don't you worry. It's not going to happen. Dad didn't mean he wants to come in and look at you in the shower. He wouldn't ever do that—would you, Steve?"

Steve appeared rattled, completely bowled over by the conversation. "Well, no. Of course not. I love you, Teddy. I would never hurt you."

"Honey," Molly began. "Daddy just asked if he should turn off the water because he's really concerned about the waste of water and how expensive it's getting. He wouldn't really barge in and turn it off on you. It was just a manner of speaking."

Teddy seemed to be calming down, but the burst of fear he had felt was obvious. Molly hugged him. It was a long, warm hug, an attempt to erase some of the ugly mistrust he had learned so young. She hadn't had to know at such a young age how dangerous life really could be. And even now, as a mother, she was just beginning to learn to mistrust family members. *Family*! The word had always meant safety before; now it meant danger. Dark and dirty games. Secrets.

"Honey, is there a reason Daddy's comment upset you so? Do you want to talk to someone about this?"

Teddy recoiled. "No! I'm OK. I don't need to talk to anyone."

Steve approached Teddy and clasped one of the boy's hands in both of his own. "I'm sorry, Ted. I didn't mean to scare you."

Teddy shrugged. "It's OK."

When Teddy had gone back down the hall, Molly asked Steve, "Why don't you hug the children anymore?"

"What do you mean?"

"You always hugged them and played with them when they were little. But you don't hug them anymore. When you're telling your sons good night, it's not natural to shake their hands instead of giving them hugs and kisses like normal fathers do."

"I don't know, Molly."

"I want them to feel loved," she said. "They need your acceptance and your hugs. You're always so distant. Is it so hard just to put your arms around them and hug them?"

"I don't know, Molly." Steve turned his back to her and ran his fingers through his hair in a gesture that told Molly he was getting upset.

"So why can't you hug them?" She pressed for an answer.

"Because I'm afraid!" He turned to her, and she saw that his eyes were brimming with tears. When he spoke, his voice was strained, choking. "Molly, I don't know what's normal. I don't want to be like my father, but I don't know what's normal!"

"Well, it's normal for a father to hug his boys," Molly said. "It's necessary. It's not secret touching—you see people hugging all the time! It's normal. It's wonderful. Your boys need it."

He was beginning to cry. Guiltily, Molly went to him and circled his neck with her arms and raised her face to his. He kissed her softly, locking his hands together around her waist. "I'm sorry," he murmured into her hair.

"Maybe I should be sorry. If you weren't married to me, you'd probably have far fewer hassles," she said thoughtfully, before unclasping her arms and making her way to the kitchen sink. She knew sleep would be a long time coming that night, as so many concerns churned around in her head.

Molly considered finding a therapist for Teddy, but he insisted he didn't need therapy, and the search seemed exhausting. "I kept him safe," she reasoned. "He's just affected by what happened to Megan."

But the troubles never seemed to stop.

One day, when she was picking up in the boys' bathroom, she came across a crumpled yellow sheet of paper on which Teddy had written a poem. It was Teddy's hastily scrawled handwriting, there was no mistaking that. But the words to the poem! Where had he come up with such vulgarities? It wasn't like him to talk that way. The poem was nasty, with references to the "noises you made when you sucked on my—."

Concerned that these were the words to a song he was listening to, she was seized by anxiety again. She felt weak and shaky; isolated. There was no one she could talk to about this. Steve would come apart. Teddy would be angry if she brought it up. She had told none of her friends about the family secret. She thought that perhaps if she could encourage Teddy to talk about the music he was listening to, he would share something about the poem with her. But she wasn't sure she could draw him out like that. Teddy was becoming more and more of a stranger of late—moody and withdrawn, with raging outbursts of sarcastic words when he became angry. And the simplest things angered him: the volume of the TV, the clutter in the car, having to repeat a mumbled statement. His anger worried Molly. Was it simply the tough teenage years, or did he need psychiatric help? If so, what was the next surprise she could expect? Would this roller coaster never stop?

CHAPTER

14

April 1984

April. A warm sun poured in through lemon yellow sheers at the kitchen window. Molly stood in the middle of its brightness with her hands in warm, soapy dishwater, methodically cleaning the plates and silverware from breakfast and wondering how long she could make the job last. The boys were at school, Steve was on a job, and she had the afternoon off—all alone with this beautiful day. But a letter from Barbara sat half-hidden under the stack of mail on the counter. She didn't want to read it. Just knowing it was there had already dampened her mood.

At last Molly was finished with the dishes. The water gurgled down the drain as she wiped off every inch of the butcher-block counters. Then she dried her hands and reached for Barbara's letter.

Standing by the counter, she read the letter quickly. There was nothing new. Lloyd was "doing well" in his therapy—getting in all his assignments and making "great strides." Barbara was in a support group for wives of child molesters. She wrote that after hearing about the beatings some of the other wives had received from their husbands, she felt lucky that Lloyd was so kind to her. If the other women had stayed with their husbands, then she certainly had no excuse to leave Lloyd.

As proof of Lloyd's generous spirit, he had bought her a new dining-room set with hutch. He had also bought a camper, and they were planning an extended trip across America. They were looking at plans to remodel the house when they returned, and their friends had taken them out to the symphony on two different occasions that week—life was wonderful!

Molly shook her head. Something was horribly wrong. Life was wonderful for the senior Bowkers, but the junior Bowkers were in deep despair.

Barbara's letter went on to say that she was driving up to see Grandma Feldman and Aunt Vera before she and Lloyd left on their trip. She knew Grandma Feldman was planning on making a short visit to Steve and Molly's; Barbara said she planned to come for a visit at the same time.

Molly sorted quickly through the rest of the mail, hoping to find something that would make her feel better. She came across a thick envelope from a counseling center in San Francisco. Feeling her pulse throbbing at her temples, Molly took the letter over to the recliner and sat down before opening it. Her hands were unusually shaky, and her throat was knotted with tension. The letter was addressed to Steve, but she read it anyway.

Dear Mr. Bowker:

   I am writing to inform you that your father, Lloyd Bowker, has been in therapy at our center for the past two months. During that time he has been in group and private therapy, undergoing a series of tests, including lie detector tests and sexual arousal tests in relation to pictures of children.

   I regret to inform you that your father is one of the most manipulative and devious clients we have had for some time. Initially he denied having molested any children, but said he was in therapy just because his children said he should go, and if that was what it took to get them back, he would do it. He failed the first two lie-detector tests we gave him, though, which showed he was being deceptive. The other clients were tough on him, and eventually he confessed to molesting more than 60 children over the past 53 years.

The letter went on to give more details about Lloyd's perversion and what initiated it. Then it continued:

I am enclosing a list of the children he kept record of in his computer journal—first names only, with dates of incidents. Perhaps you can identify some of them as family friends. You will notice that one of the children is a boy whose name he didn't even know, whom he picked up off the streets of New York on a business trip six years ago. You will also notice that none of his own children or grandchildren are on the list. I think he is lying about that, and will insist on further testing to confirm this.

Your father was easily aroused by pictures of naked children. Because of that, I must recommend that you continue to keep your children from him for their own safety. As part of his therapy, his wife, Barbara, is to keep him away from children at his church. Also as part of his therapy, he is required to write you a letter of apology. It will come in the mail soon.

Please call me if you have any questions.

By the time Molly finished reading the letter, she could hear nothing but the sound of the blood coursing through her head. The room grew dark around her, and, paradoxically, she felt weak with relief—like a person who has observed disturbing symptoms and finally gets a firm diagnosis. For years she had belittled herself for thinking the worst about Lloyd. Now she could dismiss the fears that she was being paranoid. The suspicions she had had about Lloyd *were* true. He *was* a child molester—and not only in the dark and distant past, but also in the present.

Molly put her hand over her mouth to keep from sobbing. "Oh, God," she whispered. "I brought my children there in spite of my fears. If only I'd listened to myself, no matter how impolite it seemed."

She thought of all the years she had insisted on seeing Lloyd and Barbara for Christmas because it seemed like something a good daughter-in-law would do. The thought made her furious with herself. Slamming a kitchen cupboard door closed, she screamed "You fool!" and her voice echoed in the empty house. She leaned her head against the cupboard and cried. "You fool," she whispered.

Molly dreaded sharing the shocking news about Lloyd with Steve, but he had to know.

That evening, after supper, Steve stood beside the counter and leafed quickly through the mail while she cleared the table. "What did my mom have to say?" he asked, shaking the blue envelope by a corner.

"Nothing new; just the usual. Before she and Lloyd go on their cross-continent trip, she's coming up to visit—when Grandma Feldman comes." Molly began to run the water in the sink, her fingers tensing around the dishcloth. The sun had left the windows, and now the room was shaded.

"When's she coming?" Steve asked rather disinterestedly as he fanned out the rest of the letters.

Molly thrust her hands into the soapy water and answered, "Next month." She washed and dried three Ziploc bags.

Steve looked up, and his eyes locked with hers for a long moment. "I hate it when she comes," he said, shaking his head.

"I know. So do I. But the kids need to see her."

"Maybe." He returned his attention to the stack of letters. "What's this one from the treatment center?"

"That's from your dad's therapist." She didn't want to have to talk about it now.

"How's he doing?"

"Oh, not as well as your mother thinks he is."

Steve raised his eyebrows in surprise, and Molly said, "I think you'd better sit down while we talk about this."

"Oh, no," Steve said, suddenly pale. "I don't think my gut can take this."

"It's important," Molly said. She rinsed her hands and dried them, picked up the letter, and led Steve to the family-room couch. "Sit down," she said gently. "I'll tell you generally what the letter says, but you'll want to read it yourself."

"I don't think so." He was leaning forward, his elbows on his knees.

Molly hushed him. "You need to read it. What it says is . . ." she couldn't think of any delicate way to say it. "Well, what it says, Steve, is that your father *is* a child molester. He was molested by a farmhand when he was six, and he began molesting other children when he was thirteen. When he first started therapy, he lied about it. But when they got him to tell the truth, he confessed to molesting more than sixty boys and girls over the past fifty-three years."

Steve's head dropped till his hands covered his face. Molly went on. "He kept a list of them. You might know some of these children." As she began to read the list slowly, Steve mumbled a last name and the town the child was from. He spoke toward the floor in a hollow voice that revealed deep anguish. When Molly had finished, they sat in silence for a few minutes before Steve raised his head and looked at her. Disbelief and shock had so altered his face that she hardly recognized him.

He said, "Dad was molesting my friends, and nobody said a word! Nobody said a word about it!" His voice grew louder, more intense. "Why didn't they do something? Why did they let this go on and on? They *all* were enablers—my mother and the whole church! Why didn't my mother leave him and take us away from him? Why wasn't he disfellowshiped?"

"Try to remember the times," Molly said, attempting to calm him. "Nobody would have believed the accusation. Your family has always been one of the pillars of any church they've ever joined; that was their cover. Nobody would believe anyone who said he molested their child. Even your mother wouldn't have believed, I'll bet. That's why she stayed with him."

Steve stood up and began to pace, rubbing the back of his neck fiercely. He turned suddenly. "Are Teddy and Jerry on that list?"

"No. Neither are you."

"He's lying," Steve said through clenched teeth.

"About the boys?"

"About me. I can't put my finger on it, but I know something happened between him and me that wasn't right. How about Megan—is she on the list? Or Brittany?"

"No."

"He's lying!" Steve shouted. "He's got to be lying."

"I don't know," Molly said slowly. "After Grandma Feldman's warning, I tried to protect the boys. I think I did. I hope so. And they're not on the list. I hope he's not lying." Her eyes scanned Steve's face, hungry for reassurance. She was suddenly nervous, uncertain that her boys were untouched. "But if he's not lying about Megan, then Chad and Paige are. I can't believe *they* lied to us."

"They wouldn't lie; he would." Steve sat down again, his head in his hands. "Oh, Molly," he cried, "when is this going to end? When is all this going to end?"

"I don't know," she said, and moved over to sit close beside him and run a reassuring hand over his back. She didn't, however, think he felt any more reassured than she did.

On a Tuesday afternoon in May, Steve picked up Grandma Feldman at the bus station. He couldn't contain the awful news of the truth about his father; the minute they were on the highway heading home, he asked her if she had heard about him. She nodded and then said, "And it sounds like he's up to his old tricks again."

"What do you mean?"

"Paige called me just last week. Her mother knows one of the families in the Crescent City church. They told her Lloyd molested one of the young boys in his own church last week."

Steve glanced over at his grandmother before returning his eyes to the road. "You mean, even though he's going to therapy?"

"I'm afraid so."

"It makes me sick, Grandma. This just makes me sick. Are they going to do anything—press charges or anything?"

"No, I don't think so. They don't want to cause trouble for your family."

"But Lloyd has caused trouble for theirs!"

"Well, it's a much bigger problem if the police get involved. They're afraid that the negative publicity might ruin the church's reputation . . . and your parents'. They feel that God will avenge in His own time."

Grandma Feldman reached out a gnarled hand to squeeze her grandson's arm. Her weathered face revealed a smile. "Everyone must do what they think is right," she said. "Perhaps that family doesn't want their son to go through the stress of talking to the police and of perhaps being put on the stand at a trial."

"I guess you're right," Steve said quietly. "I hope I never have to make that decision. But how do you think that little boy feels when he sees Lloyd read Scripture and sing solos at church and knows that man did something wrong and isn't being punished? Doesn't it present a horribly warped picture of right and wrong to the child?"

"It probably does," Grandma Feldman agreed. "But we can't do anything about it."

"Grandma, I'm sick of the silence. Molly and I can't visit my home church anymore because Lloyd is there. We can't attend functions at the school there anymore because Lloyd will be there.

"I can't even stand to go to college reunions. Every time I go, someone asks how my parents are. Saying that we're estranged and I haven't seen them in a while makes me terribly uncomfortable. It makes me look bad—like the uncaring child.

"He's the pervert, and he's free, while the rest of us are restricted."

They drove in silence the rest of the way home and put the conversation behind them.

When Barbara arrived the next day, it was to a cool reception. Molly dreaded talking with her. She couldn't wait till Steve got home from work. It was impossible to have a real conversation with Barbara anymore. Everything was kept shallow, touching surface issues only—news about church members moving or having babies or getting married, details about the remodeling job, their plans for a trip to Hawaii sometime after they returned from this cross-country drive.

Eventually, Barbara pulled out a little photo album in which she carried pictures of their new camper. Though Grandma Feldman was sitting in the living room with them, Molly asked her directly, "How can you stand to be with him, knowing what he's done?"

Barbara sat back as though hit with a fist. She pasted a polite smile on her lips and then lightly replied, "Because I love him."

"Even though he has hurt all those children?"

"He was just showing affection," she returned stiffly.

"Child molesting is not showing affection," Molly said. "It's perverted and evil. It's grounds for divorce. It's adultery!"

"I don't agree," Barbara said, snapping the book shut and stuffing it in her purse. "I know you and Steve want me to stop loving Lloyd, but I can't. I made a vow to love him in sickness and in health, for better or for worse. He's a sick man now, and I won't leave him."

"Even if it means not seeing your grandchildren on a regular basis?"

The corners of Barbara's mouth were twitching, and she patted her stiff curls nervously. Again making sure she had the pasted-on smile in place, she replied, "The Bible says that God won't give me anything I can't handle. Since He has given me this, I know I can handle it. And I will."

Molly cut in. "Barbara, you're misquoting that Bible verse. It doesn't say God won't give you more trials than you can bear—it says *'temptations.'* God won't give anyone more temptation than they can bear, but will always provide a way of escape. The Bible says that Lloyd was given a way of escape—each time he was alone with a child. But Lloyd never took that way of escape. He even chose to go ahead and molest a child last week! His therapy hasn't worked, Barbara. Can't you see that?" Molly stopped herself, hearing the anger in her words.

Shifting in her seat, Barbara said earnestly, "I wish you could see Lloyd lately. He's a different man—so gentle and kind. Our marriage is the best it has ever been. His therapy has made such a dramatic change in him already."

"Barbara, we're not asking you to stop loving him; a person can't always turn love off. But open your eyes; look what he's taking from you! He's committed adultery with over sixty children—over sixty unconsenting children—many of them more than once. He is a *homosexual rapist!* And you're staying? Would the pastor allow Lloyd to teach a class at church if he had raped sixty women in the church? No! Not even if he had had consenting affairs with sixty women. And yet, because his victims were children, you are all winking at this as though it's just 'a little mistake.'

" 'He's sick,' you say. 'He can't help it.' You feel sorry for him. Well, he's not sick, Barbara. He's a cold and calculating criminal. He chose to hurt these children—he stalked them first and lured them into danger. And you're not doing him any favors by protecting his crime. *You've got to separate the crime from the sin and treat each one appropriately.*"

Barbara began to fan herself, then picked at the hem of her skirt. Molly continued trying to explain: "Barbara, I'm glad you feel happy. That's something I haven't felt for some time now— sustained happiness, that is. Steve and I have been on an emotional roller coaster for the whole sixteen years of our married life. We can't take in foster children and show them love because of Steve's problem with drugs. Whenever I've agreed to help out with some function at church, something happens at home that so depresses me, I can't participate. We're living in an unstable environment. We can't see our friends at your church because Lloyd is there. Your church is as good as locked to us because of him—because of the silence, yours and that of that boy's family. Why don't you do something? Why don't those of you who can, do something to protect the as-yet unmolested?"

Barbara's hands were shaking, and her face was flushed. Molly suddenly felt sorry she had been so outspoken. Placing a hand over Barbara's, she said, "I'm sorry I've hurt you. But this has been very difficult for Steve and me. Our lives aren't going as well as yours. We are still paying for Lloyd's mistakes."

The boys' entry couldn't have been better timed. "Hi, Grandma," Jerry called, flinging himself onto the couch beside Barbara. Grandma Feldman held out her hands to Teddy, the deep creases in her face etched into a smile. "Hi, honey," she said, pressing his cheek to hers.

"Are you staying for supper?" Jerry asked.

"Yes!" Barbara replied happily, ever the actress. "Grandma and I are leaving in the morning."

"Well, you better watch me on my skateboard now, before Dad gets home and we have to eat supper," Jerry said. "Come on!" He stood up and hauled his grandmother off the couch, and Molly hurried into the kitchen to make supper. While she berated herself for talking so bluntly with Barbara, she also felt angry that Barbara had chosen to continue to wear the plastic face that denied that her "perfect," fairy-tale family was flawed. Why couldn't she see how awful her husband was? How could she stand to sleep in the same bed with him?

The conversation limped through supper as Barbara recounted for Steve what all the church members were doing.

Finally, Steve put down his fork and managed to say with a shaky voice, "I don't want to hear about the church members, Mom. I want to hear when you're divorcing your husband."

Barbara appeared stunned. "You're asking too much. I don't want to lose my house," she said helplessly.

"Aren't we more important to you than a house?" Steve asked in astonishment. "And why should you lose the house? *He's* the one who needs to be kicked out. He can get an apartment. I can't believe you can let your children and your grandchildren slip out of your life so easily. Don't you want us to visit again? Mom, we can't come home again as long as he's there!"

Barbara wasn't making sense. Grandma Feldman and Aunt Vera had said it was because she had been brainwashed, and Steve found himself inclined to agree. Somehow, he had to get her away from Lloyd.

In the morning Barbara and Grandma Feldman left to drive to Grandma Feldman's home in Astoria. That night, Steve had his first terrifying flashback. He remembered, for the first time—in living color—everything his father had done to him. He could smell the oniony, greasy odor of the motel and see the grimy yellow walls and the orange bedspread in the room he and his father shared. Again he knew the terror he had felt as he awakened to find his father's hand in his underwear; again he heard the weak explanation, "I was just checking to see if you have to go to the bathroom." Again his chest constricted as he saw blood on his underwear and wondered if he was bleeding to death. And again he remembered what it was like to have no one to talk to. He was haunted by the silence, by the gleaming rows of white teeth set in closed grins that kept the silence and pretended everything was all right. This must be what every little boy feels like with his dad, he had reasoned. This must be what fathers do. "No!" Steve bolted upright, yelling into the night.

Molly woke up with a start. "What's wrong?"

"Nothing . . . everything . . ." He moaned deeply. "I'm thirty-five years old, Molly, and I just remembered. What a nightmare! . . . I was molested too. Every single night, I woke up with an erection, and his hand was in my pants. Every night! When I went on sales trips with him, I *had* to sleep in the same bed with him, with him behind me cuddled next to me like two spoons. My preference to sleep alone was never honored. He forced himself on me." Steve was choking back sobs. "I hate him!" he cried sadly.

"You can't hate him, Steve. It'll kill *you*—not him."

"I know, but I can't help it. I hate him. He drugged me, and then he raped me. That's why I got hooked on that Demerol so easily. That's something child molesters commonly do; they were talking about it at therapy. You remember how stocked Mom's medicine cabinet was with Percodan and Phenobarbitol—she passed them out like candy. She's probably on Valium now; that's why she's so strange."

Molly nodded. It made sense now. Steve kept rambling, his eyes glazed. "I can't forgive him, Molly. He's nearly ruined my life, and he hasn't had to pay anything because of it! He just keeps on doing it to others. Think of the other lives he's ruined—the lives of my friends and even children I didn't know. Why didn't Mom protect me? Why?"

"I don't know."

It was a question that might never have an answer. Molly guessed it was a matter of self-preservation—that Barbara so feared darkening Lloyd's mood that she allowed him to do anything he wanted; that she was willing to sacrifice the emotions of her children for what she saw as "peace." Let the dragon have his way, if it will make him hold his fire.

Steve said, "I've been so blind. I resented your mistrusting my dad when the boys were little. And when you insisted on taking Teddy to the bathroom yourself when Jerry was born, I thought you were overreacting. I was so stupid, Molly—so blinded by the ugly ways of my family, I couldn't see danger like you could. I didn't realize he was abnormal, but you did. And now I'm thankful you saw through him."

Did I really? Molly wondered, and then said, "Minimizing or normalizing the abusive ways of one's family is pretty common. We studied about it in psych. Unless you make yourself believe what's happening in your family happens in normal families, you would have to do something drastic about it—and drastic changes are scary."

"I know."

"As a little child, you needed to feel safe with your parents, so you 'normalized' what they did. But now—with distance—you can see that something very evil was happening in your home. It scares me to think how 'normal' your family seemed, when you were all, in fact, unstable."

"I know," Steve whispered again, wiping his eyes. He turned his pain-racked face to hers and caught her soft cheeks between his hands, then tenderly kissed her mouth. "Oh, I love you so much. I don't know what I'd do without you."

"You'd have somebody else," Molly assured him. "You might even like her better." A glimmering wish that someone else had been dealt this hand flitted through her mind.

Restlessly, Molly fluffed up her pillow and tried to return to sleep; but sleep wouldn't come. At last, when Steve's breathing became even, she climbed out of bed and stumbled to the bathroom. Leaning against the sink, she held a towel to her face to keep from screaming, "Why? Why? Why?" There were no answers.

Finally, after crying herself into exhaustion, she crawled back into bed and slept.

It was still dark when Steve woke the next morning from a restless sleep, his haunting memories still fresh on his mind. Pursued by the evil demons of his past, he dressed quickly in the darkness, dashed off a note to Molly, and hurried to the car. He drove 14 hours straight, stopping only twice, until finally he pulled up at the office where his mother worked in Crescent City. He had to tell her his memories and toss the demons at her feet. She needed to know before she left on a trip with that man!

Barbara looked up in surprise when Steve shadowed her

doorway. "I've got to talk to you," he said urgently. "Where can we go?"

She stammered, with a big, engaging smile, "Oh . . . OK. We can talk in the lunchroom."

For the first time, Steve told his mother in painful detail how he had been molested as a child. He connected incidents that had not made sense before, but had suddenly come together in this awful, twisted puzzle. He asked her to divorce his father and make her house safe again. And he asked that, until she divorced Lloyd, she not visit for a while—it hurt him too much. "You didn't protect me," he said. "This really happened to me. I'm not making it up, Mom. I was molested, and you didn't protect me, and I'm feeling really angry right now. I need some time to sort this out."

Sitting on the edge of the table, Barbara listened numbly, her face as devoid of emotion as if she hadn't heard a thing he said. Talking to her was like talking to a mannequin.

Finally, Steve realized that she was not going to give him the validation or support he was seeking. "Aren't you going to do anything?"

Barbara had no reply. She just stared through him as though he were a window.

"I'll go then." Feeling lost and empty, Steve raised his hand in a shallow farewell and left the demons with her.

She responded, at last, with her plastic smile and a promise to drop Molly and him a line while she and Lloyd were on their trip.

"No—please don't write," Steve said. "I don't want to hear how wonderful you think your husband is or about all the fun you're having. I'm not having any fun, Mom. . . . Excuse me, but *this is hell*."

She let him go as though he were a stranger, without even offering him an embrace. Steve's heart was heavy. If she wouldn't believe him as an adult, what likelihood was there she would have believed him when he was a child? He found a motel and called Molly. "The trip was worthless," he said.

Molly squeezed her eyes shut, hoping Steve could feel all the love she had for him. "I love you. I believe you," she said softly, knowing the words didn't take away his pain.

"I love you too. I'll be home tomorrow," he promised.

Molly hung up the phone and thought of Barbara. How could she just watch while her own children and grandchildren were being brutalized by her husband?

Lloyd's required letter arrived the next week.

Dear Steve,

I'm sorry for anything I may have done to you. I certainly didn't mean to hurt you. I was just showing affection. If you think you've been hurting, just think of how your mother feels. She wouldn't have had all the ulcers she's had over the years if you hadn't done the things you did. I only hope you can find it in your heart to put away all the anger you feel toward me. I have done nothing but show you affection all of your life. And if you felt I was hard on you, it was only because I cared about you, and whatever I did was necessary for you to learn your lessons.

Molly shook her head and stuffed the letter back into its envelope, knowing it was going to make Steve angry. But she hoped that confronting his mother might have given him the control he needed over this situation. It had been good to find a logical reason for his drug abuse. Now that the unseen cancer was gone, he could work on healing.

Steve's therapist wanted Steve to get his anger out of his system, so he assigned him to write a letter to Lloyd sometime during the next two weeks. It took him ten days to complete. He began by typing the words, "Lloyd Bowker." No greeting; just the necessities. He added another line, and then abandoned the project with a sense of despair. Molly watched helplessly as he lingered often at the typewriter on the desk beside the refrigerator, brushing the keys with his fingertips.

A week later, Molly was tidying up the kitchen late one night when Steve came plodding in, looking disheveled and ashen. He walked over to stand beside the typewriter. The letter was due in just two days. "Are you going to finish that now?"

she asked, hoping he would. She hung the dishrag over the sink.

"I should. But it's so hard, Molly. You don't know how terrifying this is."

"You'll feel better if you write it," she urged, drying her hands.

Steve's face twisted. He looked like he was going to bolt. "I don't think I can, Molly!"

"Why not?"

"I don't know!" He sounded panicked. "I'm . . . I'm afraid!"

"Afraid of what?" she asked gently.

"I'm just afraid. He'll be so angry." He rubbed his eyes with the heels of his hands.

"But what can he do, Steve? We're miles away. You're not a child anymore; you're a big man. You don't have to be afraid. You have a right to feel what you feel; a right to be angry; a right to tell him so."

"I don't know," he said desperately. "It feels so wrong."

Molly caught his glance and held it. "But it's very right," she said firmly.

Steve turned and left the room. Soon Molly heard the shower running. She went to the bedroom and prepared for bed, picked up a magazine, and crawled between the sheets. When Steve finished his shower, he found reading material of his own and slipped into bed beside her. They read in companionable silence for quite a while. Then, sighing loudly, Steve laid down his magazine. He sat on the edge of the bed for a moment, his head in his hands, then heaved himself to his feet.

"Are you going to do it?" Molly asked quietly.

"I don't know."

Molly heard his heavy footsteps all the way down the hall. Worried, she slid silently out of bed and, at a distance, followed him to the kitchen.

Steve sat at the typewriter. In slow motion, he turned it on and scrolled in a sheet of paper—the letter he had started. Then, leaning forward, he dropped his head to his hands and moaned.

"Do it, Steve," Molly urged. She put her hands on his shoulders and massaged them gently. "Don't be afraid."

"I'm so scared," he whispered.

"It's OK. You're safe."

Finally, he began typing. Then, turning his agonized face up toward hers, he asked hesitantly, "Do you mind if I do this alone?"

Molly replied, "No—that's OK. I'll go back to bed."

In a few minutes she heard the typewriter keys clacking with an urgency born of desperation. An hour later, Steve reappeared at the bedroom door with the letter in his hand. A sad smile of relief was on his face. "I *did* it, Molly. And I feel so good. You can't believe how good I feel, as though a big, festering sore has just been drained."

"Steve, I'm so proud of you."

"Would you read it, please?" he asked her.

"I'm sure it's fine," she said hesitantly.

"No, I'd like you to read it so you know how I feel."

"OK."

She read quietly to herself.

Lloyd Bowker.

I have put off writing this letter because it has made me so stinking sick to think of all the rotten, filthy things you have done to me and so many other people. My marriage is just about on the rocks because I have not been able to come to grips with what you did to my life. You brought me up fearing your wrath and anger for what were simple, normal childish behaviors. I wanted to love you but found myself hating you more and more as I grew older and wiser. You made me feel I could never do anything right.

The letter continued with specifics about the abuses Steve remembered. Then Steve wrote:

You can tell me about all the good things you did for me as I was growing up, but all the money and things of this world cannot make up for the lack of true, heartfelt love that you should have had for us children, or for the self-esteem that you took away from us through your perverted sexual appetite.

Through your sick, perverted behavior, you taught us

that it was OK to lie, to cover up the truth, to hide the truth from our own wives. We grew up covering up for you. We grew up learning to lie our way out of any and everything that we did wrong or thought you would think was something we did wrong. Remember, 'This is our little secret, and we don't want to tell Mom.' You may not remember saying that, but you did in so many different ways.

Having said this, I feel much better. I feel like the sewer that has been rotting in my mind is starting to empty out. You filled it, and now it's time some of it returned to you.

Molly lifted her eyes to his and smiled warmly. "You did it," she said, realizing the strength it had taken him to write it. "You're healing."

After Barbara and Lloyd received Steve's letter, Barbara called and asked if Steve wanted to be disinherited.

"No. I didn't ask to be disowned," he said. "If that's how you feel about me, I guess it's your right. But I was just letting you know how I feel—for once."

Steve told Molly later, "I guess I'll probably be the only one left out of their will. I seem to be the only one who remembers being molested; and I'm still paying, aren't I? I'm still the 'bad one.'"

"You're not bad," Molly assured him. "You're the only one with enough sense and strength to think for yourself and stand up against evil. We don't need their money. We'll be fine."

Grandpa Feldman died just before Christmas. Steve and Molly wanted to go to the funeral, but Aunt Vera said Lloyd was insisting on coming to support his wife, so they stayed at home. Being with Lloyd was too difficult—seeing his moods, feeling his domination, hearing his cutting remarks, being reminded constantly of what he had done to his family and to so many other children. It had been a year since they had seen him, but Molly still startled and stiffened whenever she saw a man who resembled him or who talked in the syrupy voice he used. She regretted that Lloyd's presence was keeping them from what should have been bonding events for the Bowker family.

Things were going smoothly for Lloyd—no arrest, continued outings with friends, continued status in his home church. Molly wanted to send postcards to each member in Crescent City, warning them that Lloyd was a molester; but that would have been libel and could have gotten her in trouble with the law. Her hands were tied; there was nothing she could do. Why didn't the victims do something?

Molly missed having family around. It seemed a lifetime ago that she was happy and secure in the family in which she grew up—a lifetime since she had had all of life before her and the expectation that it would continue to be full of enjoyment. The reality was that for the most part, her sixteen years of married life had been tumultuous. Only by sheer determination had she stayed married. She didn't like the changes she was seeing in herself as a result of staying. *I've learned to mistrust people*, she realized. With her trust in Steve a fragile, broken thing, she had become wary, sometimes cynical, and not as accepting of others as she once was. It made her sick to realize that Lloyd had affected her in this way.

She had become uncomfortable with the pious at church and with those who took the relatively easy lives they had as evidence of God's favor. Their logic suggested her suffering was a sign that God had chosen to distance Himself from her, that He was frowning on her. *Had* she lost His favor? Surely not. Molly came to regard such theology as shallow and self-serving. It wasn't a fair God who would sprinkle only certain favorites with blessings while allowing the pain of others to go on and on.

She had slowly come to see the blessing her struggles had brought. They had brought a blessing by prompting her to search desperately to understand Jesus . . . to get her priorities in order and raise her sights to higher ground—the next life, where things would finally be fair and just and perfect.

In searching her Bible for guidance on how to deal with her anger toward Barbara and Lloyd, Molly had scribbled Bible verses on a number of scraps of paper. She decided that she would start keeping a serious journal of her communication with God. As she learned to know Him better, her heart continued to warm to Him.

CHAPTER
15

October 1984

On a brilliant October day in Seattle, Molly purchased a journal that provided needed therapy. The rains had polished the streets and the naked trees during the night, turning the bare branches into glossy black filigree against the startlingly blue sky. Molly loved autumn. It signaled the beginning of winter, when nature took the time to heal and rest before growth began again in the spring. Molly needed a winter of her own, a season to heal. She breathed deeply of the fresh air as she guided her car to her favorite store, The Book Shelf.

At Molly's request, the clerk pointed out a rack of quilted journal books. "These are particularly lovely," she said.

Molly agreed. "I have one for each of my boys. I write in them on their birthdays," she said. "Love letters—kind of—to record what they're doing and what they get for presents. That way, if I should die before they really know me, they'll always know how much I loved them." Molly was thinking of her offer to be a sacrifice if God should need her to die to shake Steve up. But she couldn't tell a stranger about this; she wouldn't understand.

"That's lovely," the clerk said pleasantly. "So now you want one of your own."

"Right." Molly selected one with a cover of pink tapestry roses, purchased it, and returned home.

Blissfully alone in the house, she sat down with her Bible and pulled out the scraps of paper on which she had been recording her thoughts. Now she could organize them and write them in her journal.

151

Molly's very first entry was Hebrews 10:26, 27. This passage showed her a God she could agree with. It was her opinion that the God most often presented from the pulpit was one-dimensional—too tolerant. Such a *laissez-faire* God was exactly the kind a child molester would like to believe in, but that kind of God offered little comfort to angry victims. Molly loved the Old Testament God, who was hard on sin, who meted out swift and sure punishment to evildoers. It was difficult for her to believe that the Son of the Old Testament God could be soft on sin.

The second passage she entered was 1 John 5:16, 17. She had had numerous frustrating discussions with the people at church about different degrees of sin. "Even we as humans can tell the difference between involuntary manslaughter and pre-meditated murder," she had said one day in a discussion at church. "I think there are different degrees of sins too."

"No," one saintly little woman had rebuffed her. "The Lord says if you break one commandment, you are guilty of breaking them all. Sin is sin. There is no sin greater than another."

"I think your interpretation may be wrong," Molly had said gently. "I agree that all sins are equal in the sense that they all separate us from God. But some sins are more grievous than others, and consequently, they require a more severe punishment than others."

Molly's comments sparked a huge debate—which she regretted. But nothing anybody said changed her mind. The conclusions at which she was arriving increased her appreciation of God's fairness.

Just a few minutes remained before the boys would be home from school. With her Bible open in front of her, Molly knelt in front of the couch and buried her face in its soft cushions while she whispered a prayer into the fabric. Then, placing the Bible and the flowered journal beside the lamp, she went outside to pick up the mail.

The sun had made its cameo appearance for the day and was now obscured behind steel-gray clouds that were scudding across the sky at the mercy of a whipping wind. The straggling yellow leaves that had refused to fall till now were spiraling wildly to the ground. Molly shook her hair from her eyes, hurried to the mailbox, and then back to the house before the rains could begin again.

In the stack of letters, the Crescent City church newsletter caught her eye. It was almost a given that each newsletter would contain some disturbing news from that church. In a recent issue, Molly and Steve had read with knotted stomachs Barbara's report on the dedication of the Crescent City church. Lloyd had sung a solo to commemorate the event. Molly and Steve both felt that a child molester should not be honored in such a way. Molly had written to the pastor and expressed her concerns, but had received no reply.

Molly read through her other mail, saving the newsletter for last. As she leafed idly through it, her eyes fell on a picture of Lloyd and Barbara with some other members of the church. The caption beneath the picture read: "Crescent City Organizes RV Club." Under the photo was an article that Barbara had written. Molly scanned the article, freezing at the last line. "The RV Club hopes to provide a ministry to the single-parent families in the Crescent City church."

Lloyd! Trying another angle. This was his idea—she was sure of it. How convenient for him to befriend fatherless children and be a "father figure" to them, winning their confidence and then destroying their souls by molesting them.

It would happen. Lloyd's therapist had said child molesters— the professional term was *predatory pedophiles*—were incurable. Especially when they had been practicing their perversion all of their adult lives. Two Christian psychiatrists and a psychologist had confirmed this to Steve and Molly, one of them explaining, "Lloyd is turned on by children in the same way you are by members of the opposite sex. It is as unlikely that his sexual preference will change as it is that either of you will become homosexual. A normal man flirts with women; a pedophile flirts with children. The difference is that a woman can say No or do something about the seduction; a child is taught to always say Yes to adults and is therefore vulnerable."

Molly knew she had to say something. Crescent City had a new pastor; perhaps he would listen to her. So Molly sat down at her typewriter and wrote him a letter. Choosing each word with care, she revealed Lloyd's record of child molestation—including the fact that he had even molested his own granddaughter. She told the pastor of the therapist's warning that Lloyd would always be potentially dangerous. She asked the pastor what effect he thought Lloyd's prominence in the church must have on his victims and said the church's silence empowered him to continue victimizing the church's children. She closed the letter with an appeal to the pastor to protect the vulnerable children of the church by warning their parents and by using appropriate church discipline. Molly added her address to the bottom of the letter, hoping for the courtesy of a reply. But she never received one.

The next week Dr. Woods, who had been the Bowkers' family physician when Steve was a child, surprised Steve and Molly by stopping by for a visit. Dr. Woods and his wife were retiring and moving to the small town of Manzanita along the Oregon coast, where he would see a few patients and operate a small practice. They were visiting a few of their friends along the way. Cory Woods, the doctor's youngest son, was a friend of Steve's, and they had gotten Steve and Molly's address from him.

After supper, Steve steered the conversation to his problems with his parents. "My dad has molested his own granddaughter," he told Dr. Woods. "I just don't understand how my mom can stay with him. I can't get her to see how dangerous he is. Do you know if this is a surprise to her?"

"Oh, it's no surprise, I'm sure," Dr. Woods replied. "When you lived in Pendleton, your dad was doing this. I told your mother then that the only treatment for him was castration or female hormones. She thought he'd get better, and I thought since they've lived in Crescent City for so long that he must have. I didn't know it was still going on. This is . . . what . . . thirty some years later?"

Steve nodded. "He molested me. Did you know that?"

"I'm sorry. I didn't know," the doctor replied.

"His friendship with you was a good cover; it made him seem honorable, I guess," Steve said. "He had you all fooled. He was even molesting Cory—did Cory tell you?"

"No!"

"I saw Cory on alumni weekend last year and told him the truth when he asked about my folks. He said he was molested too, but had never told anyone about it. You'd be surprised how many of my friends have revealed that they were molested by him; yet their parents have continued to be friends with my family all these years! What's wrong with everybody? Why didn't they believe their kids and do something about it?"

"They didn't want to hurt your mother," Dr. Woods said. But that was not a good reason for silence. By avoiding the issue, they had only postponed the hurt and allowed it to grow much larger.

During the two years after Steve confronted his father, life settled into a comfortable routine for Steve and Molly. Steve's drug dependency vanished, and Molly began to trust him again. Those two years were the longest uninterrupted period of relative happiness in their eighteen years of marriage. During that time, they moved from Ballard to Edmonds—where they purchased a small, comfortable home with a big front porch and a welcoming swing. Every fall, the row of alder trees along the back fence provided a striking panorama, their leaves taking on the look of glittering, golden coins. Molly took advantage of the cheering view by opening all the curtains on that side of the house.

Steve found a permanent landscaping job in Edmonds, with a delightful boss, and gave up thoughts of teaching at the university. Molly cut back her work schedule, working only every other weekend. She still felt uncomfortable giving patients shots of Demerol—the drug that had nearly killed her marriage. On her days off, she volunteered as a teacher's helper at the church school. But she still found time for a regular browse at the immense Goodwill store in downtown Seattle, where she bought nearly all the family's clothes—as her mother had done years before.

Life was finally going quite well. The only concerns that still troubled her occasionally were the Crescent City church's cover-up of Lloyd's perversion and Teddy's continuing restlessness.

At the end of the past summer they had enrolled Teddy in a Christian boarding high school south of Crescent City—the same school from which Steve had graduated. This, his freshman year, marked his first extended absence from home. Molly missed Teddy, who, now that he was in high school, preferred being called Ted, and she hoped everything was going well. Like a typical teenage boy, Ted seldom wrote.

Late one February afternoon, Jerry was curled up on the couch, reading. Molly stood by the counter, sorting through the mail while Steve hurried in and out with kindling and logs for a fire. It was cold—even for February. They had enjoyed lunch together with friends after church and ended up staying the whole afternoon. Now they were home. It was nearly dark outside, the street still and shadowed and the sky in the afterglow of sunset streaked with long scarves of coral.

Molly hoped for a surprise letter from her sixteen-year-old son. None had come. But there was a letter from Lloyd's therapy group in San Francisco. "Do you want to open this?" Molly asked, holding the letter toward Steve.

"No—I'm not up to that. You read it," Steve said.

Molly tore the letter open carefully. It was a thick letter—two letters, really—one from Lloyd's therapist and another in Ted's familiar scrawl. She shivered as the words from the therapist rose up to meet her.

Dear Mr. and Mrs. Bowker:

Lloyd Bowker, who remains in treatment here, brought the enclosed letter to me last week. He is required to do so as he can have no contact with you or any of your family without our (and more importantly, your) permission.

My reason for sending this is not, however, to discuss Lloyd's rules. As a parent myself, I feel you should know of your son's obvious psychological distress. His rage may lead him to harm himself or someone else. I recommend he be seen by a competent mental health professional, as he appears too fixated to get on with his life.

Should you wish to discuss this or any other aspect of our treatment program, please feel free to call me.

With trembling fingers, Molly straightened the copy of Ted's letter and began to read, editing the profanity as she went along.

Dear _____. (The obscene name Ted used made Molly sick.)
I have only one main point to make to you: I hate you. How dare you accept any people to your house, especially my friends! I _____ hate you. How dare you show them my baby pictures. I hope you didn't claim me to be your grandson, because I'll never be anything to you.

I hate thinking about what you did to my dad. If my dad doesn't get revenge for what you did to him, I will. I swear it. I don't care if I burn in hell with you, I'll get you. I will get revenge. You don't mean _____ to me at all. All you are to me is another _____ child molester. ____! That's what you are. You always will be. I hate having you as my relative, as my "grandfather." If I ever find out that you did to me what you did to my dad, I will kill you. There are no words that can explain my hate toward you. The only punishment that will satisfy me is death.

Because of you I have become an extremely hateful person. I hate everyone. I trust no one. I believe in nothing. My faith in God is depleting. Right now the only reason I live is so I can see you die.

I've turned unbelievably racist. The swastika is my banner and my way of life. I hope soon to join a skinhead gang somewhere around there. If you don't already know, one of the kinds of people skinheads hate and will kill are gays and child molesters.

You have got to be the worst type of person alive. You overpower young children, boys and girls, just to get off sexually. I remember explicitly when you tried to molest me. I won't go into details, since details aren't necessary to make you remember. I do remember that more than just once you tried to do that _____ to me. I despise you so much I wish God would kill you now so I could get on with my _____ life.

I hope this letter lets you know exactly how I feel toward

you. What I've stated here also reflects my brother's feelings toward you. If I ever find out you touched my little brother, the punishment that you will get from me will be so _____ horrible you will wish you weren't alive.

The letter went on, asking Lloyd to call so Ted could express his hate to him personally. It was signed, "Burn in hell, Ted Broker. That's right, I changed my name."

The letter left Molly paralyzed with shock. "Oh, God," she murmured, "what do we do now?" A suffocating sense of guilt washed over her. She should have insisted he see someone three years ago, when he and Steve had words about his lengthy showers.

"What's wrong?" Steve asked.

"Ted wrote a hate letter to Lloyd. He's angry about what your father did to you. We've got to call the dean." Molly's voice revealed the panic she felt.

It took several minutes to reach Ted at the dorm. When Molly heard his cheery voice on the other end of the line, she felt somewhat better.

"Am I in trouble?" Ted asked warily.

"No, honey. We were just worried about you. Got a copy of the letter you wrote to Lloyd. His therapist thought you might be so angry that you'd hurt yourself."

"Oh, that," Ted said, chuckling. "I was just trying to scare him."

"What brought it on?"

"Oh, after Christmas vacation one of the girls who lives in Crescent City was walking in front of me on the sidewalk here at school. She said, 'Hey, Teddy. You were a cute baby.' I said, 'Thanks. But how did you know?' And she told me, 'I went to your grandpa's house over Christmas, and your grandpa showed me all your baby pictures.' When I got back to my room, I was so angry that I wrote the letter. Is he going to call me?"

"No. He's not allowed to have any contact with you. But, honey, I'm worried about you. I don't want you to be a skinhead."

"Oh, Mom. Don't worry. I just said that to scare him so he'd be sorry for what he did to Dad. Nobody in the church will own up to the fact that he did wrong and that they hate him. But the skinheads do, and I like that."

"Teddy, what he did to Dad is in the past. You can't change history. It's awfully sweet of you to want to fight Dad's battles for him, but it's not necessary. It takes too much energy. You use your energy to study and to have a good time. As far as changing your name—that's fine, honey. You can call yourself anything you want to."

"I don't want anyone to link him with me."

"I don't blame you. But you don't have to carry his shame, Teddy. Tell what he's done. Tell that girl he's dangerous. Tell her he's a child molester—Daddy doesn't mind. The only way you can take the shame off your shoulders and put it back on Lloyd's is by telling. And that's the only way we have of protecting others. So tell. Daddy doesn't mind." Molly's words came out fast, breathlessly.

"I'm not going to tell. But I do wonder . . . did he do anything to me, Mom?"

"No, honey. Thanks to Grandma Feldman's warning, I protected you. He didn't hurt you." Inside, her stomach twisted.

"OK." He sounded unconvinced, but Molly was confident she had kept her eyes open as he was growing up and visiting there.

"Now, don't just go around angry. Talk to the counselor there at school, OK?"

"Maybe. But I'm fine. Really."

"OK, honey. I love you a lot. You're very, very special."

"All right, Mom. Don't worry about me. I'm fine."

Molly placed the phone carefully in its cradle, replaying their conversation. How could she be so certain Teddy wasn't molested? There were a few times he was in the radio room with Lloyd. But when she had checked on him, she had found nothing out of the ordinary. It was impossible Lloyd had gotten his hands on her son. But if he had . . . what would she do?

A phone call from the school the next month heralded the beginning of more trouble. Ted had been suspended for smoking. They drove to the school and picked him up. Seeing him outside at the picnic table, a cigarette hanging from his lips, wrenched Molly's heart. Who was this person she called her son? He had become a stranger. He disappeared for long periods of time during the day and came home reeking of tobacco. Yet there was still a gentleness about him. Each evening before he went to bed, he made sure he kissed her good night, and he would clean the kitchen without being asked when he saw that she was tired.

Once again Molly experienced the helpless anxiety she had suffered while Steve was addicted. Ted couldn't return to school until he had quit his smoking habit. She prayed for guidance as to what would best help him.

In time, Ted promised to attend stop-smoking classes. His extended spring vacation seemed extra long and stressful, but he returned to school smoke-free.

Four weeks later, Molly's roller-coaster ride took another unexpected and shocking twist. The phone rang at eleven o'clock at night. It was the boys' dean. Molly and Steve were both on the phone, instantly awake.

"Um, Mr. and Mrs. Bowker. This is the dean. I found Ted walking around outside the dorm tonight. He and I talked, and he has something I think he should tell you."

Molly's stomach knotted. Was somebody pregnant? Had he started smoking again—or drinking? Was he on drugs?

There was crackling on the line as the phone traded hands. "Mom." Ted's voice was a whisper.

"What is it, honey?"

"There's so much pressure, Mom. I just want to be dead."

"Honey, don't talk that way."

"But it's true. I just want to be dead. I want to kill myself."

"Ted—" Molly shot a worried look in Steve's direction.

"Mom, I didn't want to tell you. I don't know how to say this. But Lloyd . . . he got me."

"He what?" Molly asked in a tight voice.

"He did it, Mom."

"He molested you?" Molly held her breath, feeling her stomach flip over. Steve swung his legs over the side of the bed, the knuckles of his hand whitening as his grip on the receiver tightened.

Ted was sobbing. "I shouldn't have let it happen. I'm such a fool! I didn't want to tell you because I knew I'd break down. I'm so stupid! I hate myself . . . I hate crying!" He was gasping for air.

Molly could hardly believe it, could hardly breathe. But she would not doubt her son. "Honey, it's not your fault," she assured him, struggling to fit all the pieces of the puzzle together quickly, guessing at how it happened. She wanted to scream. Instead, she kept her voice as calm as possible. "You didn't *let* it happen—he forced you. And that explains the letter you sent to him?"

"That was when I started remembering, when that girl talked about him."

"What did he do, exactly?"

"Does it turn you on to hear all the details?" Ted sniffed in irritation.

"No, honey. I just want to know how badly he hurt you."

"He touched my privates, Mom. In his radio room. The Christmas he gave Jerry and me the pogo sticks."

Steve's breath was coming in short puffs. He cut in urgently, as though he had suddenly reached a conclusion.

"Ted, I'd like to report this to the police. Is that OK with you? You'll have to give a statement and talk to them about it, but he's got to be stopped. OK?" Molly stared at Steve, surprised that they had both reached the same conclusion at exactly the same time.

"When are you going to call?" Ted asked in a little-boy voice.

"First thing in the morning. I'll drive down there to be with you. You're going to be OK, Ted. I'm glad you told us," Steve said, running his hand through his hair.

"You want the dean now?"

Molly said, "Yes. And you get some sleep, honey. Everything's going to be all right. I love you so much."

The pressure inside Molly's head was immense—she felt as if she were going to burst! She wanted to be with her boy to hold him and make everything all right, but she couldn't. No one could ever make this all right. A piece of their son—his trust—was missing, taken away permanently. They could never get all of it back. Why hadn't someone told on Lloyd years before and spared them this? She wanted to shake the do-gooders who had kept silent—and who, by their silence, were also to blame for her family's pain. It seemed as though she was in a dream. She wished it *were* a dream. If only she could wake up and be done with it! But it was chillingly real.

Though they found it difficult to speak, they talked with the dean long enough to ask him to watch Ted in case he might attempt suicide. Then, wearily, Steve switched out the lights, and they slid down between the covers and closed their eyes. Molly's heart was lurching in her chest. She thought that if the phone rang again, she would surely lose what control she was barely holding on to. She counted her racing pulse and struggled, with difficulty, to slow her breathing.

Clutching the hem of her blanket to her chin, she fought for an understanding of this nightmare. The unspeakable had happened. Her own child had been molested in spite of her vigilance, and she was probably in the next room while it was going on. Guilty! She was the reason Ted had been molested. She was the one who had insisted they visit Lloyd and Barbara all those years. Why hadn't she listened to her own discomfort with Lloyd and kept the children away from him? But she had only wanted her boys and their grandparents to share warm memories! The stress she was feeling set her teeth to chattering. She knew intellectually that she wasn't guilty. Yet she felt responsible for taking Ted into a dangerous situation simply because she wanted to do the "right thing."

As Molly struggled to find a way to establish a measure of control in this situation, she realized the powerful ramifications of Lloyd's abuse of Ted. It was a bittersweet realization. All through the years they had begged the parents of the victims to report Lloyd, but nobody would. They said, "God will get vengeance for us." Even the pastor wouldn't speak out against him. But now . . . now they could do what no one else had had the courage to do.

Molly's temerity surprised her; where was the Molly she used to be—the Molly who was willing to let others walk all over her? That had been a Molly without a mission; a naive Molly who had had no idea what fear and anger and righteous indignation meant. Everything—everyone—was different now.

At length, Molly whispered, "Steve? Do you realize what this means?"

Steve groaned, and Molly realized he hadn't yet found anything useful from this latest blow. She said, almost triumphantly, "We're not helpless anymore."

Despite finding a positive side to the situation, though, Molly found herself staring wide-eyed at the shadows on the ceiling, fighting a suffocating sense of entrapment. And her feelings of guilt remained. Finally, she closed her eyes and forced herself to relax. What would she tell a friend who felt guilty? She would lay all the blame on the perpetrator. She began to find a sense of direction through this pain. They would work through this and make something good come from it. Ted would speak for all the children haunted by silence through the years.

Realizing this, miraculously, she slept.

CHAPTER

16

At eight o'clock the next morning, Steve called the Crescent City police. In an unsteady voice he said, "I need to report a child sexual abuse case."

His call was routed to a special detective, Emily Cox. "My son has just told me that he was molested there in your town by my father. We want to press charges."

After requesting more details, the detective asked, "Can you come down? I'll need to take your son's statement in person."

"We'll be there tomorrow," Steve promised. "I'll pick him up at school and be at the police station around four p.m."

"That will be fine. I want to reassure you—the law prevents the perpetrator from suing you for libel or slander when you report a crime, so you don't need to worry about that. Victims are usually concerned about that aspect."

"Thank you; that's good to know," Steve said.

Emily continued, "I'll go over the details of your other rights when you get here. See you tomorrow."

Ted spoke to Detective Cox for nearly two hours the next day. When they emerged from the office, Emily said that even though Ted was a teenager, they had used anatomical dolls to make it easier for him. But she would not divulge details of his statement. Molly asked, "Then he really was molested?"

Emily nodded. "It seems so."

"What happens now?"

"We're going to take it slowly. I'm not going to just rush out

165

and arrest Lloyd. We must have corroborating statements from other victims before we do that."

"He's been in therapy for several years," Steve said. "Apparently his therapist has a list of victims that he kept on his computer. We thought he would automatically be reported to you when he started treatment—and, to be honest, we have been feeling frustrated that he was never arrested. We were afraid there was some reason why he couldn't be arrested, since it hadn't happened yet."

"He couldn't be arrested if there was no one to press charges," the detective explained. "I'll ask the therapist for his file to help us in indicting him and bringing him to trial, and I'll get a copy of the list and call everyone on it.

"It may not be easy to convict him. Most of the crimes are probably beyond the statute of limitations. And we can't use hearsay as evidence, so we can't charge him for crimes involving victims who don't want to make statements. It's my job to collect statements from the victims who wish to come forward. I'll also collect any other material I can get and present it to the prosecuting attorney. If he says we can convict on what I have collected, then we will arrest Lloyd. I'll call you when that happens."

"How long will that take?" Steve asked. He explained quickly, "Molly's parents are coming next month for a vacation. We're going to San Francisco, so we'll be hard to reach."

"It could take several weeks. You might even be back from your vacation before he's arrested. If you can give me any names of possible victims who may *not* be on his list, I will also contact them to see if they want to testify."

"Oh, we can give you names, all right," Steve said.

"Good. Basically, it's the state that's pressing charges—but if victims don't come forward, we don't have a case. Judging from Ted's testimony, there are others out there who need to come forward. As to Ted's case, the timing couldn't be more perfect. The statute of limitations extends seven years from the crime and/or until the victim's eighteen. As near as we can guess, Ted was about ten when it happened, so he's under the limit— the statute has not run out yet."

Steve nodded. "Good." Then he added, "I can give you those names right now."

The next week, Ted was asked to leave the church boarding school—for smoking again. It was a bizarre, ironic situation: a church school "disfellowshiped" a teenager for a health hazard of several months' duration, while a church congregation warmly embraced a perverted adult in spite of a lifetime of sex crimes.

Back home, Ted showed Molly a book of poems he had written. They were disturbing, making frightfully apparent the serious effects Lloyd's abuse had had on Ted.

The first poem in the collection read,

I feel hate indefinitely
I feel hate toward everything I see
I love to hate, and that's a fact
I'm controlled by hatred, it's as simple as that
Hate comes very easy for me
I want to die, so I can be free
If death can come as easy as hate
I hope I die tomorrow 'cause I cannot wait
So many problems, all around
Hold me underwater, maybe I'll drown
I'd like it, but I'd wonder whether or not
Would I go to Heaven or to Hell and rot?

Molly trembled at her son's despair. She wondered how Barbara could call herself a caring Christian and then minimize a crime that had such a serious effect on its victims. Molestation was not a "little mistake." Affection? Lloyd hadn't shown affection—he had shown the children the darkest of evils and then told them he was a man of God. Was it any wonder the children wanted nothing to do with the church? Ted still had no interest in becoming a member if what had happened to him represented what Christianity was all about.

Molly shuddered. It was so wrong—what Lloyd was allowed to do. He was murdering children's souls inch by inch, destroying their innocent trust in the Lord and in His people. She lifted pained eyes to Ted's face, but he seemed nonchalant about the seriousness of the poems.

"Ted, are you telling me you want to kill yourself?"

"Oh, no. I just wrote those to shock the teacher. He wrote 'disturbing, but good use of language' across the top."

"It is disturbing," Molly agreed. "He should have showed them to someone."

"No big deal," Ted said.

"I'm making an appointment for you to talk to someone about this," Molly said. "Will you go?"

"I guess," he agreed. "But it's no big deal, Mom. They're just poems."

"But they speak volumes," Molly explained. "Lloyd has violated you, and you're angry. You have a right to be. But you also need help understanding and getting over that anger so you don't actually kill yourself."

"Don't worry, Mom. I won't kill myself."

If only I could believe that, Molly thought. She made an appointment for Ted to see a child psychiatrist the next day.

In early June, Molly received the message they had been waiting with mixed emotions to hear.

It was unseasonably hot. She was in the kitchen, preparing a fresh taco salad for supper. The boys were outside having a water fight, and she heard their playful shrieking. They sounded more like elementary-school children than fourteen- and sixteen-year-olds. But it made her smile, remembering the happier days when the boys were little and carefree, before all this had happened.

The phone rang while she was chopping the lettuce. She laid the knife on the chopping block, wiped her hands on a towel, and picked up the receiver.

"Hello?"

"Hello. Molly? This is Emily Cox."

"Hello, Emily." Molly's voice sounded distant to herself. She fumbled for a chair and lowered herself carefully as she braced for the news.

Emily was straightforward and gentle. "I'm calling to tell you that Lloyd has just been arrested—fifteen minutes ago. We have him in custody here in the city jail."

"I see." Molly felt as though a cannonball had struck her in the stomach. For an instant, she was frightened. She struggled with the feeling that she and Steve had been "bad." But as she remembered Steve's pain, and Ted's, she realized again that they had done the right thing. Actually, what they had done would help Lloyd. The first step in fixing a problem was to identify the problem. When everyone covered up Lloyd's problem, it gave him the opportunity to deny that he had done wrong.

"Was Lloyd surprised?" she asked Emily quietly. "Did you have to bring him in with handcuffs?"

"No. He wasn't really surprised—at least he didn't seem so. I called him at home and said he had been reported for child molesting and that I wanted him here at the police department in fifteen minutes. Rather than use force, we always try to ask for compliance; it makes things easier for all of us. Lloyd said he wanted to talk to his pastor and to call his therapist. I said he could, but that I expected a phone call in fifteen minutes if he was still at home.

"He agreed, and he and his wife and the pastor arrived here half an hour later. I read him his rights, handcuffed him here in the office, and took him downstairs to the jail."

Molly shivered. The news was painful, in spite of being a relief. It was impossible to feel exultant—this was family in jail. But there was a clean sense of relief, a shedding of that nagging sense of uneasiness that something wrong was not being dealt with. Now, at last, they were seeing the first payment on a long-overdue penalty. Molly felt a surprising sense of closure; she guessed it must be something like Steve had felt when he remembered his abuse.

Molly asked how Barbara had taken the news.

"She was pretty upset, more upset than Lloyd was, really. He was very submissive—they usually are when they're guilty. Barbara asked, 'Why now?' And I asked her, 'Why *not* now? For the victims, it's never over until it's reported, duly processed, and there's a resolution and justice is done.' "

Molly nodded. "Isn't it interesting," she said thoughtfully, "that now, when it's Lloyd and Barbara's time to suffer consequences, they think it's unfair? Did they really think they should get away without suffering a little?"

"I mentioned something like that to her," Emily said, "and she seemed surprised by it."

"So what happens now?"

"By law, Lloyd has to enter a plea of guilty or not guilty, and his bail must be set within seventy-two hours. I'm pushing for an arraignment tomorrow afternoon. You can come if you want to; Ted might want to be there in the courtroom to see Lloyd in handcuffs while the charges are read against him—so he can see the positive results of telling."

Molly swallowed hard and closed her eyes.

"I know this is difficult for you," Emily said kindly, "but you did the right thing. I have been calling all over the country to contact the victims on his list. It's been a healing process for them to know that he is being arrested, to hear me say that they were wronged and that justice is being done. They've been very thankful for your courage in coming forward."

"So we have other victims pressing charges?"

"The state is pressing charges. But, yes, we have other victims who have agreed to testify against him. One of them, in particular, is in college now and never told anyone until I contacted him. He's grateful for what you are doing. There are some I have contacted who don't wish to testify, and that's their right. I think we have enough."

Molly said, "I gave you the name of the town Barbara and Lloyd were living in when he lost his job. Was there any record of him there?"

"Nobody filed any charges," Emily said. "At least, the person I talked to on the phone couldn't find anything in the records. But I'm not really surprised. Churches cover up these kinds of things for their employees all the time. They think moving the criminal somewhere else will stop the problem, but it only spreads it. The people here aren't very motivated to press charges either."

"I know," Molly agreed. "Neither was Steve's brother." She

said hesitantly, "We gave you the name of Justin Harder—my former roommate's son. Was he molested?"

Emily cleared her throat. "I'm sorry—I can't give you the names of the victims. But we interviewed all the people you suggested to us. Two of them came in to talk to me."

"Then Justin was molested?"

"Let's just say your information was helpful," Emily told her. "But not everyone is pressing charges."

Molly let out an audible sigh. "Do you mean Vicki?"

"I'm not saying her son was a victim or not, but there is no Harder family pressing charges."

"It's not fair," Molly cried. "Vicki was the one who got Steve and me together. She always stood up for Lloyd. And now this. She's still sticking up for the Bowkers even though her own son was a victim. I just don't understand it!"

Emily Cox said, "It happens. Lots of people get confused about what loyalty demands of them."

"So Lloyd's being arrested for just fondling Ted?" Molly asked.

"There was more to it than that," Emily said, edging. "But there is no such thing as 'just fondling.' Even an adult's verbally seducing a minor for sexual conduct is a form of molestation and is against the law."

"Can you tell me what Lloyd did to Ted?"

"I'm sorry—I can't. I'd have to get Ted's permission first, and I don't think he'd give it. But of the statements I have, Ted's is the most incriminating. What Lloyd did to him is a class A felony, and the statute of limitations has not run out as it has for the other victims."

They closed the conversation, and Molly replaced the phone in its cradle—a confusing mixture of emotions boiling around inside her. On the one hand, she was glad that this was happening. At last she had accomplished what she had been trying for years to do: she had exposed Lloyd for the evil man he really was. His arrest would be in the paper and TV; no one could cover up what he had been doing any longer. Further abuses weren't likely to happen in the Crescent City church, at least for the next few years.

But Molly worried about the division this could bring within the family. How would it affect the relationship between Chad and Paige and her and Steve? They had planned to visit Grandma Feldman during their vacation, after Molly's parents left for home. Would Grandma and Aunt Vera be hostile? Now that they had given this most private of family secrets to the police, its control was out of their hands. If it went to trial, the whole town would know all the details. But perhaps it would provide asense of closure for Ted.

Overall, Molly thought it was the right thing to do. She remembered a biblical passage she had read recently: "Submit yourselves for the Lord's sake to every authority instituted among men; whether to the king, as the supreme authority, or to governors, who are sent by him to punish those who do wrong and to commend those who do right" (1 Peter 2:13, 14). She had written that verse in her journal just the night before, along with Proverbs 24:24, 25: "Whoever says to the guilty, 'You are innocent'—people will curse him and nations denounce him. But it will go well with those who convict the guilty, and rich blessing will come upon them."

The back door squeaked open and slammed shut, and Steve's tall frame shadowed the room. "Hi," he sang out. "Smells good." Then he came closer and looked at her. "You look like you've just seen a ghost. What's wrong?"

Molly swallowed and looked up at him from her chair. "Lloyd's just been arrested. He's in jail."

Steve nodded. The muscles in his jaw twitched, and he found a chair of his own. "Did Emily Cox call you?"

"Yeah." Molly told Steve how it had happened and what his mother had said. Their victory had a hollowness to it—after all, the person it involved was Steve's father. Along with the abuse there were some happy memories.

"I've got to call Grandma and talk to her before Mom does," he said. "And I'm calling his therapist. Why don't you get on the other line."

Grandma was surprised by the news, but still very supportive. "You did what you had to do," she said, "and I'm glad. I've seen Lloyd over the years because I said he wasn't going to stop me from visiting my daughter. But I insisted that he stay away from here when the other families came to visit; they weren't comfortable with him here, so he wasn't invited. He's been trying harder and harder to wheedle an invitation to Christmas at my house. Just last December, in fact, Barbara told me, 'This standoff needs to end.' I know she was saying what he wanted her to say. Now we don't have to worry about him coming anymore."

"So *we* can still visit you on vacation?"

"Of course, honey. You know you're always welcome here."

The response from Lloyd's therapist was just as supportive. "That's the best news I've heard since I first met the man," she said. "I've been so frustrated with the people in the church who have refused to go to the police and have allowed him this protective cloak of silence. Silence empowers the evil one. And Lloyd is the same person he was when he first entered therapy. Barbara is supposed to have been responsible for keeping him away from children while he's been coming here, but we have had no legal power to enforce that. Now we have the legal system to put some teeth into the restrictions we have made. I just wish someone had come forward sooner."

"I know," Molly agreed. "The people at the church thought that because a few of them knew about Lloyd, they could protect the children. But I suspected him. I suspected and watched carefully, and yet my own child was molested practically under my nose. He's calculating and manipulative and very, very cunning."

"That's the nature of the pedophile," the therapist agreed. "They never molest just one; and they never change.

"Interestingly, the Bible speaks to this very process your family is going through. You know about that verse in Exodus 20:5 that says the sins of the fathers reach 'unto the third and fourth generation'?"

"Yes," Molly replied.

"Ted is apparently the fourth generation—the last of Steve's family to be affected by the grandfather's sins. Studies have proven that it commonly takes four generations for child abuse within a family to be dealt with and stopped. It's very possible that Lloyd's father was the first generation in that family to molest a child. He never sought help. Lloyd is the second generation, a person who used his own abuse as an excuse for perpetuating the crime. He didn't seek treatment until he was forced to. Steve is the third generation, the first one to choose to stopthe cycle of abuse. He didn't remember or deal with his father's abuse of him until he was in his thirties, but at that time hewas half the age his father was when he sought treatment.

"Ted's the fourth-generation victim of his great-grandfather's sin. He also has chosen not to perpetuate the cycle. And look at the age he was when he remembered his own abuse: sixteen! Again, about half the age his father was. Ted is either the third or the fourth generation affected by sexual abuse, and—if that scripture applies here—the cycle will end with him, and his children will live the kind of peaceful lives both he and Steve have often wished for. Most victims of abuse enter the helping professions, you know. They become teachers or medical professionals or counselors in order to help others."

"I'm still worried about Ted," Molly said softly. "He seems to be going off the deep end, getting into trouble and not caring."

"That's not uncommon," the therapist exclaimed. "I wouldn't doubt that his smoking is a direct result of the abuse. A child who is abused feels he is bad. He believes that he was chosen *because* he was bad. And because he was chosen, and he didn't prevent this bad thing from happening, he thinks he *is* bad. Feeling like he can't change anything, he acts out to fulfill what he thinks are everyone's expectations. Hate and rage are natural; Ted has to direct his rage toward what Lloyd has done instead of toward himself and society."

Molly let out a sigh. "How long can that take?"

"A lifetime. There are going to be trigger points in life when he may need professional help again: when he has his first relationship with a woman, when he becomes sexually active, when his first child is born, and when that child turns the age Ted was when he was molested."

Molly felt as limp as a comatose nursing-home patient. So it would not be truly over for many more years.

After talking to the therapist, Molly and Steve tried to call Aunt Vera, but she wasn't home. So Steve called Aunt Louise and asked her to call Barbara and offer support. "I know this is hard on Mom," he said.

Aunt Louise's response was surprising. "I haven't talked to Barbara in a couple of years," she said. "I was eight when Barbara and Lloyd got married. Lloyd molested me before the wedding. I'm so angry at her for staying with him and enabling him all these years that I've stopped talking to her. I can't support her through this at all."

"I'm sorry to hear that," Steve said. "I didn't know. But I must say it makes me feel good to know you're on our side."

"You bet I am," Aunt Louise said. "And I'm proud of you."

After hanging up the phone, Steve stood up and shoved his hands deep into the pockets of his jeans. "I wonder if I should call my mom."

"If you want to, it's fine with me," Molly agreed. "I'll leave if you want a private conversation."

Steve wrestled with the thought for nearly half an hour. Finally, he went to the bedroom and placed the call. He returned an hour later, ashen and obviously drained of energy. "I don't have a mother anymore," he said.

"What?"

"She reacted as though she had never heard about Lloyd's dirty secrets. She even said she asked Grandma about what she told you when Ted was born. She says Grandma denies saying anything to you." In agony, he ran his fingers through his hair. "It's as though she was hearing for the first time that Lloyd is a child molester. Something's wrong with her, Molly." His voice was thin.

"She's brainwashed."

The timing of Molly's parents' vacation seemed almost divinely inspired. Her dad, Brad, had been concerned for some time that the situation between Steve and his family was unhealthy—with Lloyd and Barbara free to keep their secret and pretend nothing serious was happening while Steve and Molly were suffering. As a fellow pastor, Brad had called the Crescent City pastor months before, when they finalized their plans to visit Molly and Steve. He wanted to visit with the pastor and ask his assistance in helping Lloyd to see how necessary a true apology was for Steve's complete healing. Brad hoped for a full reconciliation between father and son; Steve said it was impossible.

Early the morning after her parents arrived, Molly and her father drove Ted down to Crescent City for the arraignment. Molly felt a surreal, disturbing sense of distance from everything. Since getting news of the arrest, both she and Steve had had difficulty concentrating on what they were doing. The realization that she was about to see Lloyd again made Molly feel weak-kneed and light-headed as she entered the stuffy, paneled courtroom. She could feel her heart hammering wildly in her chest, and she felt pressure behind her eyes.

She followed her father toward a seat on the back bench, stroking Ted's arm as he stood beside her. He was a good boy, tall and lanky, with a shock of dark hair, dressed in a teen's standard blue jeans and T-shirt. His eyes, still big and brown, weren't as warm as they once had been; they seemed almost haunted—too serious for a teenager. Yet Molly knew the stony exterior he presented was just a shell he held in place to protect the sensitive child he was. She determined to help him shed that exterior and be happy again.

One at a time and wearing handcuffs, several child molesters were led in for their arraignments. As Molly sat through the hearings, she was surprised to find herself becoming comfortable with the system fairly rapidly. After listening to the prosecution and then the defense of two molesters within thirty minutes, she felt more prepared to see Lloyd when he was brought in. She wanted to surprise him by being there. Ted had said he was going to shout obscenities, but Molly had advised him to sit quietly. Eventually she felt a sort of identification with the other spectators in the room, who also must have been white knuckled to see the perpetrators they knew.

They sat in the courtroom for two hours, waiting for Lloyd's case to come up. When it didn't, Molly quietly asked one of the barristers if Lloyd's name was on the docket. When he checked and didn't find it, he referred them to the prosecuting attorney's office up the stairs. There, the attorney's associate told them that Lloyd had waived his seventy-two-hour rights for release and was still in jail. The arraignment would not take place that day; when it would be held was still undetermined.

"He's right downstairs," the attorney said.

Ted asked eagerly, "Can I see him?"

"I don't think I'd advise that," the attorney replied.

Back at the police department, Molly asked to see Emily Cox. When Emily saw Ted, she smiled broadly and grasped his arm affectionately. "I'm so proud of you, Ted," she said firmly. "Look what you've done for so many people! Because you were brave enough and strong enough to report this man, you've led us to many other victims who hadn't told for all these years. And they owe all of this to you."

Ted shrugged, and one corner of his mouth turned up in a shy smile. Emily went on. "I'm sorry Lloyd's arraignment wasn't today. That would have been good for you to see. Unfortunately, the attorney he chose is one of the sleaziest, most unethical ones in town. Most defense attorneys won't take child molesters and rapists, but this one specializes in such cases—and he'll push the laws to the limit to defend Lloyd."

Ted nodded and crossed his arms on his chest. The muscles at his temples twitched.

Emily warned them, "After the arraignment, my phones aren't going to quit ringing. Every news reporter as far away as San Francisco is going to want to know details. They might even find you up there in Washington—your name isn't that common. If they do call, please just say you have no comment. We don't want anything to destroy this conviction."

Molly nodded, realizing this most private of insults was mushrooming out of their control into the hands of strangers who now could comment on it, debate it, and label each of them. She wondered what other unforeseen consequences their action might precipitate.

Molly still didn't know exactly what Lloyd's abuse of Ted had involved. Wanting more details, she asked Emily, "Can I speak to you for a moment down the hall?" When they had found a private corner, she said, "I really feel I need to know what Lloyd did to Ted. He said Lloyd touched inside his underwear, but it must be more than that. You said it was a felony. What exactly does that mean he did?"

Emily nodded and swallowed. "Ted was . . . raped."

The words caught Molly off guard. It was worse than she had imagined. She stepped back slightly and groped to steady herself against the wall, feeling suddenly dizzy. Her throat became dry. The crazy thought hit her that if this were a movie, the crescendo would happen here. She swallowed hard. "By rape," she managed to whisper, "you mean . . . sodomy?"

Emily explained quickly. "Lloyd put his mouth on Ted's penis while he was playing with the computer. When Lloyd told Ted to do the same thing to him, Ted refused and ran out into the redwoods and hid."

Tears sprang to Molly's eyes, and a horrified sob escaped from her throat. She wondered, Was this before or after she had specifically given him permission to tell his grandpa No?

"He was about ten," Emily said. "I'm sorry—that's all I can tell you because of confidentiality. This man used his church membership as access to children." She clutched at the files she held in her arms. "The way he groomed these children and exploited their trust and the trust of their parents makes even my blood curdle. This is one of the most disturbing and far-reaching pedophile cases I've ever investigated."

Molly could hardly talk. She nodded and managed to say, "Thank you," before rejoining her father and Ted in the lobby. When they got into the car and started toward the church for their appointment with the pastor, Molly looked back over her shoulder at Ted, reached out a hand, and stroked his arm. Her fingers were still shaking. She managed to force some squeaky words that needed to be said: "I'm so proud of you, honey. I love you." She couldn't say anymore as she blinked back the tears. Ted turned his head to stare out the window, his mouth fixed in a straight line.

CHAPTER
17

I t was eerie to enter the foyer of the Crescent City church after an absence of several years. Molly, Ted, and Brad, Molly's father, walked down the hall to the pastor's office. The church secretary opened the door when she saw them, and Molly's throat tightened, wondering whose "side" she might be on, expecting hostility. But there was none. The woman was gracious and friendly. Ted wandered the dark halls solemnly, remembering events from the past. Then he returned to the car to wait there while Molly and Brad talked with the pastor.

The pastor said that he hadn't replied to Molly's letter of warning about Lloyd because she hadn't specifically asked for a reply. "I showed your letter to several of the elders in the church who have known the Bowkers for some time," the pastor told her. "They said the problem was under control and that Barbara was keeping him away from children. I didn't think it was any of my business to bring up his past when it wasn't something that affected me."

"I can understand that," Molly said. "This should all have come up years ago."

There was an uncomfortable pause, and then the pastor asked, "Have you considered that God may have allowed this to happen to your son because you needed to learn a lesson of some kind from it?"

Molly flinched and slid back in her chair at the suggestion. Then, recovering her composure, she leaned forward and replied firmly, "I don't think so. I don't think God is at a master control switch, choosing for some people to go through life blissfully and others to suffer because someone they know needs to learn a lesson!"

The pastor responded, "Some people will tell you that. They believe that God has a plan for everyone's life, and apparently this is His plan for Ted."

"No!" Molly said earnestly. The thought was impossible. Did God plan for the African people to starve? He couldn't possibly plan suffering. "I can agree that God has a plan for everyone's life, but His plans are only good ones. He has a good plan for Lloyd's life, but Lloyd isn't following it."

The pastor smiled. "Actually, I agree with you. But I must warn you that not everyone will. Opening this up to the public may be more painful for you. Many Christians are confused about God's role in suffering."

"I know that," Molly said. "I believe God can *use* every bad thing that happens to pull us closer to Him, but He doesn't *will* for bad things to happen to anyone. Unfortunately, He gave all of us the freedom to choose—bad people as well as good. And sometimes innocent people are harmed by the bad choices others make."

"As you have been harmed," the pastor said gently. "I want to help you, if I can."

"I appreciate that," Molly said gratefully. "And I wish other pastors years ago had had the same philosophy. The families whose children were abused should have pressed charges then and got it out into the open. Lloyd should have been disfellowshiped until he made a public apology."

"But I think it's too late for that now. And it's important for your own healing that you forgive and forget."

Molly said, "Luke 17:3 seems to indicate a prerequisite for forgiveness, doesn't it? '*And if he repents,* forgive him.' Lloyd has never repented. But even so, forgiveness doesn't mean that punishment is not necessary for the evildoer. Ecclesiastes 8:11 says that unless there is a consequence for sin, people will continue to plan more and more evil. We've seen that clearly in this situation."

"I still think God can forgive Lloyd," the pastor told her.

Molly shrugged. "I don't know. Romans 1:28 says God eventually gives people up to their depravity."

"I hate to think that anyone's doomed," the pastor replied cautiously.

"So do I," Molly agreed. "We are all afraid to face our vulnerability. And yet, the Bible says that God allows people to doom themselves." She brushed at a piece of lint on her skirt and said, "Actually, at one point it was important to me to prove to myself from the Bible that Lloyd would not be saved. But that's not important anymore. We don't really know the answer to that, and it's not worth wasting energy on. What is *not* unknown anymore is that this man is dangerous, and everyone needs to know it. Lloyd needs to experience a consequence for his sins. That is why we reported him. And that is why I feel good about what we did."

The pastor asked, "What do you think the church should do?"

Brad spoke up. "I'd like to see Lloyd take responsibility for hurting these children. I don't think a public apology is asking too much. If he could be urged to apologize and then take the consequences, I think it would help in bringing healing—not only to this family, but to all the others involved."

"Well," the pastor said, "I've talked with Lloyd about this, and I don't think that's going to happen."

"Why not?" Molly asked.

"He doesn't want to open up a can of worms. It's been some time since he molested. He's been in treatment, and both he and Barbara would rather not bring this into the church."

"But that's where the problem is!" Molly said. "He has never repented, and that is unforgivable. He shouldn't continue to be an active member. While I realize you can't make a blanket rule, I don't think child molesters should be allowed church membership in any church because of the cover that gives them and because they're incurable."

"Well, surely that's not the Christian thing to do—to ban them from membership. Perhaps not all of them are incurable. The Bible speaks of the wheat growing up with the tares, and we are not to pull up the tares—"

"Pastor," Molly cut in, "a child molester is not a weed. He's a wolf in sheep's clothing—one of Satan's henchmen, 'as a roaring lion,' if you will, 'seeking whom he may devour.' The Bible doesn't say we must allow the wolves to eat our lambs. Rather, it says we must protect our lambs. Pastors commonly tell their congregations not to report a member's sex abuse of their children because of what the negative publicity might do to the church's reputation. The pastors guard the front doors of the church while letting the lambs be hurt, and, fearing for their safety, leave by the back door. My own little lamb—my son, Ted—doesn't want to join the church because he sees it as a 'protective secret society of child molesters and their supporters.' "

The pastor leaned back thoughtfully, and Molly rushed on. "To my horror, my son has begun talking about how he identifies with the skinhead gangs because they are upfront and vocal about their hatred for child molesters. Pastor, he hasn't heard abhorrence of this crime from within the church, and he has needed to.

"Knowing about Lloyd is not enough. I knew what had happened long ago, the church elders knew it was still going on, and still there were victims. Lloyd needs to be put away—far, far away from children."

The pastor raised his hands helplessly. "I don't want our church's reputation to be ruined. I wish this weren't in the papers and on TV. We've had many new members join, and I'm just afraid that when the word gets out that we have a child molester here, it will ruin the effectiveness we have in the neighborhood."

With a helpless shake of her head, Molly lamented, "Those who want to point a finger at your church and say, 'I won't join that church because there's a child molester there,' would probably find an excuse not to join *any* church. And frankly, no one *should* join a church that supports a child molester by doing nothing about him.

"Why can't our churches be churches that protect children by reporting child molesters? Why can't they be safe places, where the shepherds can be trusted? That kind of church would be something to be proud of.

"You must be aware of 1 Corinthians 5:12, 13. That passage says the church should expel the sexually immoral person."

The pastor was looking uncomfortable but seemed to be softening. Molly continued gently, but with conviction, "If you don't think Lloyd should suffer a serious consequence, then you don't really care about him."

The pastor sat back, startled. "And you care about him? By having him arrested?"

"It's the most caring thing to do," Molly said.

"What do you mean by that?"

"Sometimes," Molly replied, "people need life-shattering consequences to shake some sense into them. If Lloyd had been reported years ago, had been arrested, and had gone to jail, he might have been shaken up enough to experience sorrow for his sin . . . and repentance . . . and forgiveness . . . and a saving relationship with God that would have led to his turning away from that sin. But instead, he was allowed to believe he had done nothing seriously wrong. Now he's still heading down a dangerous trail and taking innocent children with him."

The pastor nodded slowly. "You see Lloyd as going down a road with a precipice at the end, and nobody but you is doing anything much to stop him."

"Exactly. And we're not just shouting that he's heading toward danger; we're shooting out his tires so he's forced to stop and take a serious look at where he's going."

The pastor was thoughtful. He continued to roll the pencil between his fingers for several seconds in the silent room. It was his move. At last he said softly, "Because I'm new, I didn't realize the scope of this problem. I will write a letter to the members and explain this to them, hopefully before they learn of it in the papers."

"Thank you very much," Molly said. "This is very difficult for us, Pastor. We're not gloating or having a good time. We're shell-shocked. It's frightening to us too. But it had to be done."

"I feel for all of you," the pastor said before standing and showing them to the door.

The next week Molly received a letter from one of the women

elders in the Crescent City church:

> Dear Molly and Steve,
>   As this story unravels, it just sort of takes my breath away. I had no idea that this was going on in your family all these years. Maybe I shouldn't have written, but because of what I feel is the Holy Spirit's prompting, I decided to go ahead and offer you my support.
>   I visited Barbara when I heard about this. She asked, "Why didn't this happen 40 years ago so it would all be behind us now, and I wouldn't have to lose so much?" She said she was relieved she didn't have to live a "double life" anymore.

Molly blinked and read that paragraph again. Barbara herself wished someone had reported this when it first happened? Was she finally seeing the folly of the old ways?

> I also visited Lloyd in the jail. He said, "If this is what it takes to get my son back, it's OK. I'll do anything to have him walk through our doors again."

Molly thought, If he would do "anything" to get Steve back, he would have apologized and stopped what he was doing years ago. But he's never been willing to do any of that. The letter went on:

> You will always be in our prayers. We love you and your family, and we are hurting for you during this time. We have missed you.

In her letter, the elder had enclosed a letter the pastor had sent to the entire congregation:

> Dear Church Family,
>   With a great deal of concern and sorrow, I am writing this letter to you. As you may have heard, one of the members of our church has been arrested for alleged child

abuse. The elders of the church and I feel that we must let you know about this before it hits the papers.

No details have been released, but as your pastor, I feel it is necessary to assure you that the church does not condone abuse of any kind. As a church, we have not only spiritual responsibilities toward our members, but also legal ones. And the Bible supports this. Victims experience healing when the abuser takes responsibility for his crimes. The abuser cannot experience forgiveness until he demonstrates sorrow for his sins and a turning away from them.

To return to the situation at hand, I feel I must let you know that Lloyd Bowker has been arrested on child-molestation charges. At this point he has pleaded not guilty, and according to the laws of this country, Lloyd is legally innocent until proven guilty. As Christians, we must keep this in mind while taking precautions for our children's safety.

As more information unfolds, we must continue to show God's love to all parties involved—including Lloyd Bowker and his family. As the body of Christ, we must continue to be understanding and caring and take everything to the Lord, remembering that God's grace is sufficient in every situation.

When Molly called the woman elder to thank her for the letter, the elder said that when news of the arrest had come out in the paper, Barbara had gone around to each of the neighbors and said that the charges against Lloyd were very old, that he was not currently molesting, and that he presented no threat to them or their children.

Molly's family and her parents left on their vacation the next day. Their visit to Alcatraz took on a serious tone as they imagined Lloyd at such a facility. The roller coasters at Great America U.S.A. were even more dizzying than they might otherwise have been. With a sense of abandon, Molly even went on one that turned her upside down—a first for her. She rode it over and over again. Her old concern for safety was gone; she almost willed herself to take risks and ... maybe ... be unlucky. She desired release from life's struggles.

Too soon, the vacation with her parents was over. They flew back to their home in Michigan, leaving Steve and Molly with three more days of vacation for just their family. On their way home, they made a quick stop to see Emily Cox, the detective in Crescent City. She showed them some clippings from the local newspaper about the arrest. The truth about the evil Lloyd had done became more concrete when they read about it in print.

Steve seemed to need a father figure. He suggested they visit Dr. Woods on their way home, since his place was on the way to Grandma Feldman's. Molly agreed, hoping the visit would be just what Steve needed.

The doctor was in a meeting when they arrived, but Steve and Molly waited for an hour till he was free. They embraced him warmly, and when Steve asked to visit with him privately, Molly agreed to occupy herself in the waiting room.

Steve got right down to business. "I guess you know my dad has been arrested," he said.

"Yes. Your mother phoned me." Dr. Woods became strangely distant.

"Well, it was something that had to be done," Steve went on. "It's not been easy for us."

"I don't know why you made all of this public," Dr. Woods said, with a stern shake of his head. "It should have been kept quiet; the elders should have had a chance to talk to Lloyd about it. Why didn't you try to work something out between the two of you? With prayer, perhaps he could change."

"Dr. Woods, it *has* been kept quiet—for fifty-three years— and it only keeps getting worse! It was time to get serious about this. You, yourself, told me not too long ago that Lloyd was incurable, and that you recommended to my mother thirty-five years ago that he be castrated! Why are you saying this now?"

Dr. Woods became uncharacteristically harsh. "Your mother is suffering, Steve," he shouted, so loudly that Molly could hear him from the waiting room. "She has asked that I write a letter to the judge about the kind of man I know Lloyd to be, and I intend to do just that. He is kind and caring and doesn't deserve this. You are wrong to make this thing public! What do you suppose is going to happen now that the courts are involved? All it's going to do is ruin them financially, and it won't help any."

"Dr. Woods," Steve returned firmly. "I am not the child I was thirty-five years ago. I don't appreciate being shouted at. We've tried the silent approach, and it hasn't worked. More victims have been added to the list. Your own sons are on it. Lloyd always brought along a teenage boy to baby-sit me on the business trips I had to make with him. Those boys are even on the list. He must have had a great time with the two of us to exploit! When he came home from one of those trips, he would wake my brother up at 2:00 a.m. and 'play' with him for a while. That's not normal, Dr. Woods! But my mother allowed it. You warned her that Lloyd was perverted. You knew about it, but you didn't do anything. You're all at fault here—as 'enablers,' to use a current term."

"We didn't want everyone to know," Dr. Woods interjected.

"Yeah. That's just the problem. That was the enabling part— keeping his secret so he could keep on doing it." There was a short pause, and then Steve said, as though thinking out loud, "I had thought I could count on you to support me. I have no parents right now, and I thought you would be there for me, Dr. Woods. I am hurting too. I'm hurting deeply; and now you have betrayed me too."

The visit wasn't providing the comfort Steve and Molly had hoped it would. They left abruptly and drove stone-faced for several hours to Grandma Feldman's house in Astoria. She was alone now in the big white house on the hill that overlooked the swelling jade ocean. Aunt Vera came over, bringing her characteristic enthusiasm, and invited Steve and Molly to walk down to the garden area with her.

Barbara's bing cherry tree was in season. Molly stopped under it and plucked a few cherries, popping them in her mouth and grimacing at the brilliant bursts of flavor. They all laughed at the faces she made. Then Aunt Vera became serious and stared out at the whitecaps on the ocean for a few moments.

"What's the matter?" Steve asked her.

"You should see Lloyd now. I saw him when I visited Barbara. His attorney got him to cut his hair and shave his beard. He's been pretty spiffed up for his court appearances."

"No more Santa Claus stuff, huh?"

"No. And I'm a little concerned about the trial. One of Grandma's friends, a retired police officer, warned us that a common angle of defense attorneys is to make it seem that a child's father has molested him and then set him up to blame his grandfather, to hide the true culprit."

"What?" It was a horrifying thought.

Aunt Vera nodded a warning. "They might point the finger of suspicion toward you, Steve."

"But Steve's always protected the boys," Molly said. "They can't blame him."

"I don't know. Apparently it's been tried before and has been successful," Aunt Vera said.

Molly groaned and looked at Steve imploringly.

"I never thought of that angle," Steve said, with a worried frown. He spit out a mouthful of seeds.

Molly leaned against the trunk of the tree and hugged herself. She tried to calm herself by watching the steady rise and fall of the waves and the smooth glide of a Coast Guard ship coming back into the harbor. Like the tides, emotions—feelings—come and go, she reminded herself. This anxiety would be replaced by something else in a matter of time. But right now, the anxiety was gnawing at her, and she began to wish they hadn't reported Lloyd.

Aunt Vera chatted away, characteristically bouncing from one topic to another, and Molly was glad she had to do little except nod and chuckle politely from time to time. As she moved dreamlike throughout the rest of the day, she vacillated between feeling that maybe this stress just wasn't worth it and feeling very positive that they had done the right thing. She worried that they might have mentioned to Aunt Vera and Grandma Feldman too many things Emily Cox had told them. She knew that everything they said was likely going right back to Barbara and through her, to Lloyd's attorney. It would be difficult to stop talking freely to Aunt Vera and Grandma, but it was probably necessary. When she mentioned her concerns to Steve, he agreed to keep mum about things concerning Lloyd from then on.

Lloyd remained in jail for three weeks. When he was released, Steve began calling Emily about the arraignment nearly every other day. It was finally scheduled, but Steve and Molly were unable to drive to Crescent City because of illness. Emily called them late that day and read the judgment to Molly over the phone.

"Everyone involved in this arraignment today was amazed that it took so long," she said.

"Really?"

"Oh, yes. A procedure that normally takes a few minutes took eight hours. Barbara testified that she would chaperone Lloyd as she had been doing, and Lloyd's therapist testified that he was not a changed man and might molest again. In the end, Lloyd pleaded not guilty, and Barbara posted bail of $50,000— an unusually large sum. The judge imposed such a tight restriction on Lloyd's movements that even his trips to the bathroom in any public place have to be supervised. He is essentially under house arrest. But he's free till the trial."

Molly thanked Emily for the information and hung up the phone. She ran a distressed hand through her hair and moved slowly toward the plump blue family-room sofa, sinking gratefully into its cushions. Now they would move on to step two: the trial sometime in the misty future. She was tired of this.

Ted appeared in the doorway. "How's it going?" he asked quietly.

"Lloyd still denies molesting you," Molly said, without looking at him. With her warm palms, she tried to press out the wrinkles in her jeans.

"Well, maybe I made it up," Ted said, clenching his teeth and crossing his arms protectively on his chest. "Maybe I just have a big imagination."

Molly shook her head firmly. "No, I don't think so, honey. The signs were there all along—I just didn't recognize them. When you were ten and asked me if I thought you were gay, Lloyd had molested you and confused you. It confused you because even though he had done something you knew was wrong, your body enjoyed the sensation—so you thought something was wrong with you. But those feelings are reflexes—like when the doctor hits you on your knee. It just feels a certain way when a certain nerve is stimulated. You don't feel that way because of something you've chosen or something you've done wrong."

"He used to stick his tongue in my mouth each time I kissed him goodbye," Ted revealed with a clenched jaw.

Molly raised her eyes to his. "Oh, honey, I'm sorry. I didn't know." Frowning, she returned her gaze to the persistent wrinkle in her jeans and began fingering it again. "When you were thirteen and cried because Dad said he would turn the water off in the shower if you took too long . . . the spitting you've done, as though to get rid of some filth . . . you had started remembering, hadn't you?"

Ted shrugged. "Yeah. I guess."

"How do you feel about what's happening?" She searched his eyes warily, hoping she wouldn't learn anything alarming.

Ted's eyes became stony. "I don't feel anything, Mom."

"You seem very angry."

Ted's jaw muscles twitched, and he leaned back against a corner of the wall. "I like to be angry. It's just how I am," he hissed.

Molly was surprised by the venom. "Oh, honey. There are so many other emotions that are so much fun to feel. There's joy and peace . . . and they come when you reach out to help others. You have chosen to feel angry, because anger feels strong, doesn't it? It keeps you from feeling vulnerable. You feel in control. And you're afraid that if you give up control, you'll be hurt again."

Ted shot a look at her from the corner of his eye, his lips pulled tightly together as though drawn by a string.

Molly went on. "Emily said she needs all the evidence we can gather for the prosecuting attorney as he puts this case together. May I give her the poems you wrote last year?"

"Yeah. I guess."

"Thank you."

Ted said, "Since Lloyd denies molesting me, are you going to drop charges?"

"No."

"Well, if you do drop charges, can I press them myself?"

"Of course you could, honey. But don't worry. We're still pressing charges. We're going to get to the bottom of this. We'll visit with the DA and move forward. When we get through this, Ted, you'll feel so much better. You can really begin to live and enjoy being alive."

"Maybe . . . we'll see," Ted said tersely.

"Honey, please trust me on this," Molly said earnestly.

"I don't trust anyone, Mom."

"I know. Relearning how to trust is what the work of healing is all about."

"It's safer not to trust anyone."

Molly shook her head despairingly. "Honey. Ted. Start with one person. How about me? You can trust me, can't you?"

"I don't know."

The statement made Molly's heart ache. "Please trust me, honey. Start with me. I know I've made mistakes," she rushed on. "Some of the decisions I've made may have hurt you. But—believe me—I have never . . . ever . . . done anything intentionally to hurt you. You've got to believe that. I gave birth to you, Ted. You are a part of me, and I cherish you."

Their eyes locked for a long moment before Ted turned away with a shrug and left the room.

Molly lowered her eyes once more to the wrinkle in her jeans—but she couldn't see it any longer because of the stinging tears that pooled in her eyes.

CHAPTER

18

August 1986

The prosecuting attorney in charge of sex-abuse cases was a short man, balding in spite of his youth, whose arms were covered with black hair that curled out from under the rolled-up cuffs of his shirt. His voice was soft and gentle. And his eyes spoke volumes. They were burdened with the pain he had shared with so many victims.

It was a Sunday, two months since Lloyd had been arrested. Though it was a weekend, the attorney had made a special appointment to meet with Molly, Steve, and Ted to discuss their case.

"Pete Harrison," he said, introducing himself with a handshake and holding open the door to the deserted courthouse with his free arm.

"We're the Bowkers," Steve said.

"I figured as much. Thank you for coming," he said. "My office is upstairs."

It was a small, cramped room. Pete's yellow metal desk overflowed with file folders and newspaper articles, a picture of his wife, and a spindle full of phone messages. A long oak bookcase along one wall was stuffed with law books and assorted magazines related to psychology and criminal law. Pete pulled in two extra metal chairs from an office next door, and Ted seated himself quietly and expectantly beside his parents.

Pete shuffled through some files on his desk, selected one that was nearly four inches thick, and laid it open in front of him. Clearing his throat, he began. "I've asked you to come here

193

today to discuss what you want me to do in this case."

"What do you mean?" Molly asked.

"Well, I need to know if you want to go through with a jury trial, or if you would just as soon avoid the trial and have Lloyd plead guilty to most counts—at which time the judge would sentence him to a period of time in jail."

"How long could his sentence be?" Steve asked.

Pete read over the official jail booking. "He is presently charged with seven counts: statutory rape in the first degree—that's regarding you, Ted; four counts of communication with a minor for immoral purposes; one count of statutory rape in the third degree; and one count of taking indecent liberties with a minor."

Molly said, "Then Ted's situation is the most serious."

"Exactly. He also raped one of the other victims—several times over several years, in fact. But unfortunately, at that time it was classified as a misdemeanor rather than as a felony, and we have to charge under the law as it stood at that time. These offenses are all felonies now; he'd be locked away permanently if we were able to prosecute him under current law. But the statute of limitations has run out on those instances anyway, so there's nothing we can do about them.

"However, when that other victim was sixteen—that's about five years ago—Lloyd was still preying on him, making sexual comments to him, forcing him to look at pornography, touching him through his clothing, and trying to seduce him. That's what 'communication for immoral purposes' and 'taking indecent liberties' mean. And those are misdemeanors."

"So, how long might he be in jail?" Steve asked again.

"Well, provided Lloyd agrees and pleads guilty on *most* counts—he'd have to plead guilty to raping Ted, that one's not negotiable, and also to three or four of the other charges—he would serve six to twelve months in jail and complete all probation requirements. Those requirements could be whatever you suggest within reason, including treatment and monitoring."

"So he would continue with his therapy?"

"Yes. And I would demand electronic monitoring, at least for a year."

Molly said, "As part of his probation requirements, I think he should have to reimburse us for treatment costs."

"Absolutely," the attorney agreed. "That's always mandatory."

"And he should be prevented from leaving the state and from stepping foot onto any school campus for the rest of his life. And we want all of Steve's childhood mementos and the pictures of Ted that we gave them. It was the pictures that brought this up in the first place."

"We could ask for that," Pete agreed, and scribbled a note in the file.

"Now, what if we want to have a trial?" Steve countered. "What would the penalty be if he were convicted?"

"Oh, he'd be convicted, all right—at least on most of the offenses. If he were convicted of all offenses, his sentence would range from forty-one to fifty-four months. And that's in prison—not jail."

"In protective custody again?"

"No. There is no protective custody in prison. But I should tell you that protective custody isn't as wonderful as it sounds. We keep all sex offenders in protective custody because the other prisoners can't stand them. The burglars and murderers rape child molesters, so we keep all the child molesters and rapists in a group together. They're not the nicest of company. And they have limited free time, limited TV time, and limited access to reading material. They spend a lot of each day in their cells. As it was, the three weeks Lloyd spent in jail in protective custody were very difficult on him. He hyperventilated and thought he was having chest pains and was really uncomfortable. A year in jail is going to affect him—I'm sure of it."

Molly touched Ted's arm. "What do you want, honey? Do you want a trial, or is it OK with you to just have Lloyd plead guilty and be sentenced?"

"I don't care," Ted said stoically, but Molly saw that the muscles along his jaw were twitching. He shrugged. "I guess if we could avoid a trial, it would be better." He got up suddenly and said something about needing to get a drink of water.

While he was gone, Molly asked the attorney, "Are we certain we have a strong case? Ted was wondering if perhaps he just imagined this."

Pete shook his head. "It's not uncommon for a victim to wonder if he fabricated the whole thing, but I'm convinced he hasn't. What we have is a pattern of behavior on Lloyd's part. Ted's description of the abuse reads practically the same as those of the other victims." He leaned back in his chair and shook his head again. "No. Ted's not making anything up. Even Lloyd's attorney, when he saw the statements, agreed. He wasn't so convinced before, and he asked Lloyd to take a lie-detector test. In it, he asked Lloyd if he had molested Ted, and Lloyd said No."

"And was it a lie?" Molly wondered.

"We think so. The test determined that he was telling the truth about every other question. But every time he denied molesting Ted, the needles went off the scale. So we think there's no question about it. Lloyd's attorney, who was present during the polygraph test, realized at that time that this was going to be a very difficult case to defend. He saw the scope of his client's perversion very clearly. He told me it wouldn't be a matter of *if* he was going to jail, but for how *long*."

Remembering Aunt Vera's concern that Steve might be implicated, Molly asked the attorney what the chances were.

Pete Harrison raised his shoulders in question. "Why would Lloyd's attorney want to bring that up? Once he called Steve to the witness stand, I could use Steve as a witness against Lloyd, and that would only make our case stronger. No, Lloyd has such a stack of papers against him, that's just not going to happen. I wouldn't worry about it."

Steve said, "Well, I don't mind being a witness."

"If you're a witness, you can't be in the courtroom during any testimony, and I think you'll want to be there. I don't see, at this point, that we'd need you to be a witness. But we can subpoena both of you so you will get paid leave from your jobs. We'll put you up in a nice hotel here in town and give you a meal allowance—make you as comfortable as possible."

"Thank you."

Ted came back into the room and sat down quietly.

Pete Harrison closed the file, and his shoulders rose as he took a big breath. "You don't have to make a final decision about a trial or a sentencing at this time. I'll tell you when we really have to know."

"Thank you," Molly and Steve said together. Standing, they shook the attorney's hand.

Pete Harrison escorted them silently down the stairs, and they walked to their car without saying a word—each one absorbed in a dizzying spin of emotions. Molly realized that the self-deprecating label she had placed on herself of being mistrusting and cynical was wrong. She didn't mistrust *everyone*. The people who had impressed her as unsafe were, indeed, unsafe. She had learned to believe her instincts when something seemed odd. She had become more discerning.

But the whole situation still made Molly sick. She felt pulled in so many directions; so many worries and anxieties gnawed at her! Was raising a family this frightening for everyone? A statement she read somewhere came to mind: "All happy families are alike; unhappy families have their own kinds of unhappiness."

Lloyd had made it hard to be proud of the Bowker name. Sometimes Molly felt she wore it as a scarlet letter. It always made her shiver a little when she called the prosecuting attorney's office and realized that her married name was now a very recognizable name on the criminal record. Each time she called, she had to specify that she was not the wife of the accused but the mother of one of his victims. Still, she and Steve were determined to do all they could to bring honor to the name their boys would carry for the rest of their lives. Steve was once again using his musical talents, accompanying a community chorale in Edmonds with which Molly sang and performing with confidence an occasional piano solo when they were on tour. Molly was proud of the strides he had made. She still prayed for his threadbare relationship with the Lord.

Steve's lack of the close relationship with Jesus that she enjoyed puzzled her. Then one Sunday she had so many loads of laundry to fold that she turned on the TV to occupy the time. Sports programs bored her. Most television shows did, for that matter. And the dim-witted commercials in which the biggest problem someone had was whether her kids' socks were as white as they could be irritated her. If only life were that simple. She flicked through the cable channels, stopping when she came across a televised seminar by a Reverend Robert Denton of Akron, Ohio, the executive director of the National Organization for Victims' Assistance. The seminar was so interesting that Molly took notes. Denton said, "There are two very important paradigms, or world views, that are shattered for victims and that must be put back together for them. The first one is 'I can trust people.' And the second is 'God is love.' "

Molly thought that perhaps this was the answer to Steve's empty religious life. That night as they lay in bed reading, she told Steve what Denton had said. Then she asked, "Why don't we kneel down together before we go to sleep and pray with each other out loud?"

Steve was hesitant. "Uh, if you want to, I guess."

"You don't seem to like the idea."

"No, not really," Steve agreed.

Molly was frustrated. "Why not, Steve?"

Steve didn't have a reply.

"Talk to me, Steve," Molly urged. "Please tell me what you're thinking." She promised him some safety: "You have a right to your opinion, whether I agree with it or not. I promise I won't argue with you."

"OK," Steve said somewhat petulantly. "OK. I guess ... I don't know, Molly. I guess I *am* resentful. I resent both my mother and God. My mother didn't take care of me when I was a little boy; and even God wasn't there when I needed Him! God could have done *something*—He could have paralyzed Lloyd's hands or made my mother listen to me or *something*— so I wouldn't have been hurt and Ted wouldn't have been hurt. But He didn't! How can I believe in a God who lets people like Lloyd molest little children? How can I trust Him?"

"Steve," Molly said in a pained voice. "You can trust Jesus if you look at things the way He does—at the big picture. Jesus is on your side. We've got so much in common with Him, Steve. His major battles in life were with the hypocrites in the church; so are ours. He had a trial to worry about; so do we. When God's children in Noah's day were hurting each other, Genesis 6:6 says God was sorry He had made them because they caused Him such pain. We know about that. You and I both have said we didn't think raising teenagers would be as painful as it is. God understands, Steve. He empathizes. He's angry at what Lloyd's done."

Steve nodded silently, but Molly wasn't sure she was convincing him. "Trusting is healing, Steve. You have learned to mistrust both humans and God, but you have to get over that." As she spoke, she remembered an analogy that had come to her during one of her private worship times.

"Have I ever told you my analogy about the war that we're in?" she asked Steve. "That bad things just happen to some people in spite of God's goodness?"

"No," Steve replied.

Molly was ashamed that she hadn't ministered to her own husband. She blamed the neglect on expending her energy on her own search to understand. But now that she had grown so much closer to the Lord and had found so much in common with Him, it was as though she had passed through the rapids and was now in smoother waters, where she could reach out better to others—especially to Steve.

"I guess I see life as being a war, Steve. We're in the middle of a war between good and evil. As in any war, some people slide through, unaffected personally by the horrors of it all. Others become casualties: some are killed, others are maimed or scarred. But none of these people was personally chosen by the Commanding General to be hurt—it just happens!

"God is allowing the war between good and evil to play itself out right now. Sometimes He does step in and prevent bad things from happening. Those interventions are miracles, and because they are miracles, there is no explanation for them. But most of the time, life just happens. Eventually, the war will end, and God will rescue us and give us all medals for our suffering. Does that help you understand?"

"A little," Steve admitted, seeming to accept her explanation. But he remained reluctant to say prayers at the bedside out loud.

One afternoon in October, after one of Ted's sessions with the psychiatrist, Ted told Molly the doctor wanted to see her.

"I feel Ted's made some great strides in the brief period of time I've been seeing him," the psychiatrist said. "I think he finally has admitted that his anger belongs with Lloyd and not the whole world in general."

"I'm surprised he's been so upset by this," Molly said. "He didn't suffer a lifetime of abuse."

The doctor corrected her. "Even a single instance of abuse can cause the damage that a lifetime of abuse causes *if the child must keep it a secret.* Telling is the first step toward recovery."

Molly nodded. "I didn't realize that," she said. "But I'm glad he's understanding where his anger belongs."

The psychiatrist said that in spite of the strides Ted had made, he seemed unwilling to talk further about his feelings. They agreed to discontinue therapy until after the trial, and even then they would continue it only if Ted seemed to need it.

Molly spent much of the next week wondering whether they should press for a trial or just agree to a sentencing. Why was it that everyone talked about having one's "day in court"? Was it really that desirable? With that question on her mind, and frustrated by getting only bits and pieces of the details of Ted's abuse, she decided one afternoon to call Teresa Duncan. Teresa had at one time been a good friend of the Bowkers. Her husband had even helped build the now-infamous "radio shack" where most of the molesting had occurred.

Molly picked up the receiver and called information for the phone number. Then she dialed it hesitantly. The phone rang three times before Teresa answered.

"Hi, Teresa. This is Molly Bowker."

There was no response from the other end of the line, and Molly feared Teresa might be hostile. She explained quickly, "I'm just calling to express my apologies for what Lloyd did to your boys. Lloyd raped my son, and we have to decide between simply having him sentenced or having a trial. We've told the attorney that we probably just want to have a sentencing and have him go to jail for a year and avoid a trial. I wondered if you had an opinion."

There was a long sigh on the other end of the line. "I figured your son was a victim," Teresa said. "And I want to thank him for coming forward. I had no idea my Joel was a victim till Emily called and asked to speak to him—he's twenty-one now, you know. But Emily said Lloyd had reportedly molested young boys, and she wondered if he had a statement to make."

"And he did?"

"He was shocked that anyone knew about it. But right away he said, yes, he did have a statement, and they set up a time to talk. I said I was coming in with him. He agreed to that, so I heard everything."

"What did he say?" Molly asked. "I'm so frustrated because I didn't go in with Ted. I've just gotten bits and pieces about what happened."

"Oh, Molly, it was horrible. He molested Joel over a period of eight years. He performed oral sex on him and then made Joel do it back. And when they were done, Lloyd made Joel kneel down and pray—to ask forgiveness from God for sinning with another man!"

"Teresa—no!" It was worse than Molly could have imagined. "He told the boys they had sinned?"

"Oh, yes. He said God couldn't possibly love them unless they prayed and asked forgiveness. I just wish I could have helped him. I asked him why he didn't tell me all these years. He said it was because Lloyd told him nobody would believe him."

"Oh, poor little boy," Molly said with tenderness.

Teresa went on. "We want a trial, Molly. Joel wants to sit in that witness chair and tell everything. Our boys need to get it out of the closet. They need to hear the courtroom gasp at the atrocities and validate that they were violated. It may be difficult, but they need to tell."

"You think so?"

"Definitely. What does your boy say?"

"He doesn't really have an opinion. Of course, he's five years younger than Joel, but I think he'd like to avoid a trial."

"He doesn't know what's best. Press for a trial, Molly. It will be the most healing thing for your son."

The prospect still made Molly feel weak. "I'll think about it," she promised.

Over the next several weeks, Molly mentally replayed her conversation with Teresa, wondering if they should press for a trial or just a sentencing. Steve didn't have an opinion, so Molly decided for their family. She called Pete Harrison and said they wanted to go for the trial. And then she began to worry about how Ted would do.

CHAPTER

19

January 1987

The day after New Year's, Ted wandered into the living room. Molly was taking down the Christmas decorations. A fire crackled in the fireplace, and her favorite Christmas tape, one by the Carpenters, lent a festive air to the morning. In silence, Ted walked over to the mantel and picked up the crocheted snowman couple that Barbara had made so many years before. He got the shaping cones, placed them in the figures, and laid them in the storage box. As he straightened, he asked, without looking at Molly, "So, any word on the trial?"

Molly didn't know. It had been eight months since they had reported the crime. She said, "Nothing yet. I've called the victim's assistant at the DA's office to find out when it's going to be, but all they can tell me is that we'll hear about it a month in advance."

"What's taking so long?"

"I don't know. Aunt Vera called yesterday to thank us for the Christmas presents I sent. She said Barbara told her it wouldn't be until after February because they were waiting for a certain judge to return to town."

"Why?"

"According to Aunt Vera, this judge has a reputation for being the most lenient toward child molesters."

"That figures," Ted said weakly. He began unwinding garlands from around the tree.

"Yeah." She remembered what Emily Cox had told them about Lloyd's attorney.

"We've got to nail him, Mom," Ted said fervently.

"He'll pay his dues," Molly assured him. "It's going to happen."

With Steve and Ted's permission, Molly began reaching out to other friends to tell about the abuse and the upcoming trial. It was so difficult to say, "My father-in-law is a child molester." She was hesitant at first, afraid they would turn away and isolate her and her family or suspect Steve of being a child molester too; but they didn't. Most of their friends—and certainly Molly's family—expressed anger at the abuse and supported their decision for a trial. Molly cherished their understanding and empathy more than they would ever know.

Perhaps they understood because of their own fears. What was chilling was that so many people she told had firsthand experience of a child molester being allowed to live without consequence, dividing a congregation's loyalties. Molly's sister Linda harbored the fear that Brittany might have been a victim—though Brittany had no memory of any abuse. Molly had learned more than she would ever have cared to know about the criminal justice system, thanks to Lloyd Bowker. And though the knowledge was linked with pain, she was glad to share coping and procedural information with other victims.

That summer would mark the twentieth year since Molly's destiny had been linked with the Bowkers—since she met Steve. They would celebrate their nineteenth wedding anniversary in August. Through counseling and many honest and sometimes painful discussions, Steve and Molly had become closer and forged a stronger bond than Molly would have thought possible just a few years before. Molly was proud of all they had accomplished in spite of the discomfort they had felt while doing it: reporting the crime, telling their friends, going to counseling. Now another intimidating step loomed large in their future: the trial. She hoped that it would wrap up this chapter of their history.

Molly began to dread the painful emotions that were sure to torture them again as Steve's family chose "sides" at the trial. Grandma Feldman, though caring about Steve, would probably sit with Barbara. Chad and Paige had said they were on Lloyd's side. And Vicki, her college roommate, had told Barbara she would sit with her. Molly realized Vicki had probably had a hard time deciding, but her decision still hurt.

She wondered if anyone would be with her and Steve through the trial. Its location made that seem unlikely. Then Molly remembered that Teresa Duncan would be there as a fellow victim's mother. They could sit together and lean on each other.

She worried too much. She had to remind herself, on a daily basis, of Jesus' advice about worrying: "Don't worry about tomorrow. Today has enough worries of its own" (Matthew 6:34). She forced herself to find something within each day to look forward to, whether it was a special thing to eat or a conversation with a friend, sleep, or just a browse through her favorite store.

In March, on a particularly depressing day, Molly stood beside the mailbox and looked slowly through the stack of letters that had come. One light pink envelope arrested her attention. It was addressed in the familiar, hurried scrawl of her other college roommate, Leona. A smile leapt to Molly's face as she expectantly tore open the letter. There was no greeting; that was characteristically Leona—getting right to the point. "Molly. I know I haven't written much through the years," Leona wrote, "but I enjoyed seeing you at Crescent City during Christmastime when you came down here. I know why you haven't been here in a while, and I don't blame you a bit. Didn't I warn you years ago? Believe it or not, I still remember with fondness the good times you and Vicki and I had at college. I don't know what's the matter with Vicki—why she can't see how foolish she is to defend Lloyd and Barbara. But I pray for you often. I want you to know that I will proudly sit with you and cry with you as you go through a very difficult but necessary conviction of this dangerous man. I'm on your side." The paper crackled softly as Molly refolded it lovingly and pressed it to her heart. "Perfect timing, Leona," she said to herself as hot tears slipped down her cheeks. "And we both know why." She raised her eyes to the sky. "Thank You, Friend," she said.

Back inside, Molly went to her bedroom and pulled out her copy of the letter Ted had written to Lloyd, rereading it. Her heart lurched when she read a sentence she had never seen before: "I remember explicitly when you tried to molest me." The words had gone right over her head the year before because she had believed she had protected Ted. Brainwashed. It seemed one's brain registered only things it knew were acceptable to the conscious mind. She could understand, just a tiny bit, Barbara's problem with reality. And yet Barbara had been told about Lloyd year after year after year and still refused to believe.

Easter came and went, and still no trial date. Ted was running with a rough crowd. He was doing poorly in school and wanted to drop out; he told Molly and Steve that high school seemed like a maze he wanted out of as soon as possible so he could get on with his life. Reminding them that he was almost seventeen, he said he planned to join the Navy after getting his GED and some community college credits. His counselor supported the decision, and not seeing any alternatives, Molly and Steve agreed.

That spring a sense of loss washed over Molly with each graduation invitation they received from children of their friends. Because of disciplinary problems, Ted had not been allowed to graduate from eighth grade. Now he would miss high-school graduation as well. Molly worried that someday Ted would realize what he had given up by dropping out of high school and wish that they had made him stick it out.

About that time, Ted surprised Molly by asking if he could go down to his boarding school for graduation weekend with Travis, his former roommate. Molly and Steve, hoping to strengthen Ted's connection with his Christian friends, decided to allow him to go.

They expected Ted and Travis to be home by 10:00 p.m. Monday night. Close to midnight, Molly was nearly beside herself with worry, pacing in the darkness of the living room. Where were they? She stared hopefully at the phone, wishing it to ring. Steve tried to calm her, but she couldn't be still.

At last, yellow headlights stabbed through the darkness over the rise at the end of the street. Then the tires of Travis's car were spitting gravel in the driveway. Molly drew aside the lace curtains at the window to be sure it was the boys. In spite of her distress over their late arrival, she smiled briefly as the yellow wash of light in front of the garage caught Ted heaving his suitcase from the darkness of the car with a lighthearted laugh. Molly hurried outside in her robe. "Where have you been?" she asked in a tight voice. "I've been worried sick about you!"

"Hi, Mom," Ted said, hugging her.

Molly refused to be sweet-talked out of an answer to her question. "Where were you?" she asked in a demanding tone.

"Um . . ." Ted hedged, looking toward Travis.

Travis waved, climbed back into the car, and drove away.

Steve came out of the house to see what was keeping them. "Where were you, Ted?" he asked firmly.

"I stopped in at Barbara and Lloyd's," Ted finally admitted.

"You what?" Molly was surprised at his courage—or was it carelessness?

"I didn't think it would take very long. I didn't see Lloyd—just Barbara. We must have talked for nearly two hours."

"What did you talk about? Did Barbara know who you were?"

Ted grinned. "I wanted to really shock her, so I messed up my hair and rang the doorbell with a cigarette hanging out of my mouth. When she opened the door, I said 'Hi.' I was really shaking, I was so nervous."

"Did she know who you were?" It had been three and a half years since Barbara had seen Ted—since that fateful Christmas of 1983, when Megan was molested.

"No. She said, 'How do you do? Do I know you?' and I said, 'You probably haven't seen me since I was much smaller.' Then she got this really weird look in her eye and said, 'Ted?' "

Molly nodded. "Did she invite you in?"

"No. She waved Lloyd away and stood in the opening between the screen door and the front door the whole time."

"What did you talk about?"

Ted shrugged. "Oh, I just told her I thought she was sick because she didn't care about seeing me or Jerry growing up. I said she might never see our kids because she preferred to stay with that pervert. I used all the nasty words I could, as often as possible, so she could see what he's done to my life, and I must have smoked about ten cigarettes in front of her.

"She said we were the rebellious ones. She called Dad a prodigal child because he won't come home, and he won't bring us all home for visits anymore. She thought we could just forgive and forget and go on as though nothing had ever happened!"

Molly listened in stunned silence. Barbara had recited the same platitudes to Ted that she had spoken to Molly years before.

Ted frowned. "There's something wrong with her, Mom. It's as though she has a force field around her, and common sense can't get in. It seems she thinks we're wild and wicked. She says Lloyd and she have been having a good time, doing a lot of traveling and eating out with Patti and Chad and Christopher and all their kids, trying to live as though life is normal for them. They've been to Disneyland several times with the other grandkids. Their friends are afraid that going to jail is going to make Lloyd have a heart attack and die."

"Maybe so—or maybe Lloyd is manipulating them with that thought."

"Yeah. Maybe. She said we're the only ones who are being unchristian about this and that she hopes we find the Lord and come back as the prodigal son did."

"Honey," Molly said gently, searching his face for a sign that he hadn't been hurt further by Barbara's words. "Barbara is wrong. No one has to make a choice between being a Christian or reporting a crime. We can do both. The Bible supports what we did."

"Exactly! I told her a kid doesn't know what the word *molest* means until he's older. I didn't know. I heard it, but it was like, 'Ted has gone to camp; Ted has gotten new shoes; Ted has been molested.' Just a couple of years ago I first really began to understand what happened to me. I asked her what she thought Megan was going to think when she gets older and realizes, for the first time, what *molested* means."

"You're right," Molly agreed. "They're not helping Megan a bit by pretending nothing bad has happened."

"Yeah. I can't wait till I can talk to Lloyd in person and tell him face to face what I think about him. I told her I'm planning to, when I'm eighteen. And I'll have my father there with me to say what he needs to say too."

"OK," Molly said.

"Well, I'm tired. Good night Mom, Dad." Ted hugged them both tightly and kissed Molly on the top of her head. It seemed that in spite of the fear Ted had felt about talking with Barbara, the visit had been cleansing for him.

How was it that the most surprising news often came on the most routine of days? Three days after Ted's return, Molly called Pete Harrison to ask him a question about the terms of Lloyd's arraignment. She pulled her white chenille robe around her waist and retied the sash while he looked up the file. Molly wandered past the guest bathroom door and made a face at her reflection in the mirror. Too many gray hairs—a sure sign of middle age. Plump cheeks where once hollows had been. Where had the time gone? She measured her life in two segments: the first, before Lloyd's influence—eighteen years of enjoying life; and the second, during Lloyd's influence—twenty years that had chipped away at her contentedness with life and taught her to regard the world as unsafe. The Steve Bowkers were all eager to put this second segment behind them and start a third segment that Molly thought of as "Life After Lloyd"—after the trial—a new life without that niggling sense of uneasiness that Lloyd was getting away with the murder of children's souls. She counted on things getting much better.

Years ago, when the realization that she was related to a child molester had been a suffocating thought, she had tucked away the family tree she had been embroidering before Ted was born. It was too awful to see Lloyd's nasty name up there with those of her parents. In the future, a new family tree would hang on the wall: a tree without a past, originating with Molly and Steve. They would begin again, as Grandmother and Grandfather Bowker seemed to have done generations before—only this time the "spontaneous generation" would produce a healthy tree, not one that was diseased.

At last Pete found the answer to her question and returned to the phone. "Well, it looks as if as long as he's in public and accompanied by someone who has agreed to be his supervisor—which Barbara has done—it's OK for him to be around children," he said. The line crackled, and Molly heard him shuffling papers. "By the way, I have some good news for you."

"You do?"

"There won't be a trial."

"No trial?" Molly didn't know whether to feel relief or dismay. What had happened? Was it because of Ted's visit? Raising her shoulder to keep the receiver in place at her ear, Molly picked up the white porcelain plates, stained yellow and red from breakfast eggs with ketchup, and carried them to the sink. Then she sat down heavily at the kitchen table.

"Lloyd has changed his plea to 'guilty,'" Pete told her.

"Then he admits he molested Ted?"

"Yes, he finally does—on the advice of his attorney." Pete sounded jubilant in a tired sort of way.

Molly couldn't believe it. Lloyd was finally admitting what he had done? "What—what brought this about?" she stammered. She ran a confused hand through her hair, tugging at the deep tangles that her quick brushing that morning hadn't reached.

"Well, Lloyd's attorney has a responsibility to seek the best deal for his client. He finally convinced Lloyd that because he flunked the lie-detector tests, he would be better off pleading guilty instead of taking this to a trial. They wanted to plea bargain and plead guilty to a lesser charge, but I understood you to say you wanted full charges pressed, so we called their bluff and stood firm, and he pled guilty to the felonies."

"And what happens by his pleading guilty?" Molly asked.

When Pete replied, his voice revealed a touch of annoyance at the answer he had to give. "Well, mainly, he benefits by avoiding prison and by getting a shorter sentence."

"What do you mean?"

"By pleading guilty, the worst he'll get is six months in jail in protective custody. He'll also be required to continue therapy for a couple of years or so when he gets out."

"Is this a good thing, then?"

"Yes, it's a good thing, really. There's no use going ahead with a trial when the defendant is agreeable to pleading guilty. It takes much of the uncertainty away."

"I guess I wanted to find out what he did to Ted," Molly said with a trace of disappointment. "I wanted him to go to prison and be 'hunted' and feel a paralyzing fear like his little victims all remember so painfully."

"I agree with you," Pete said. "And he would have known that in prison. But—"

Molly hurried on. "I guess mostly I wanted to hear Lloyd say he's guilty, and I wanted to see what Barbara does when he finally admits it."

"You will."

"How?"

"He has to confess everything at the sentencing."

"And we can be there?"

"I want you there," Pete said gently. "At the sentencing Lloyd will be required to tell the judge exactly what he did, and the judge will then read the sentence. Then you'll have the opportunity to tell Lloyd anything you want. You can speak to him, and so can your husband, and, of course, Ted. That's the victims' time to dump their emotions on the perpetrator and let him see, for perhaps the first time, what they're feeling."

Molly's voice sounded hollow. "When is this going to happen?" She wanted it to be soon.

"In about two months. We should have him in jail by the end of the summer. It's just a slap on the wrist for him, but at least it's something . . . at last."

"Thank you," Molly said gratefully. "Thank you so much."

"I just wish all of it were going so well," Pete said with caution in his voice.

"What do you mean?"

"Well, that visit Ted made to Barbara and Lloyd may make my job more difficult. It could affect the restitution I can get for you. I got a call from Lloyd's attorney. They say that Ted is just a confused child whose emotional problems have nothing to do with what Lloyd did, so they don't have to reimburse you for therapy."

"Oh, no," Molly said. "But will it affect Lloyd's sentence?"

"I don't think so. He'll still go to jail. Just tell your son not to visit them again."

"I will. And, really, whether or not we get back the money we've spent on therapy isn't that important. But we do want the pictures and memorabilia in our hands . . . and we want Lloyd to go to jail."

"All right. I'll keep you posted," Pete said before saying goodbye.

Molly hung up the phone and sat back in a daze. She had waited for Lloyd's admission of guilt for so long she felt no particular emotion. It was a hollow victory, knowing Lloyd had only pleaded guilty for selfish reasons and that he would claim he had nothing to do with Ted's anger. Pleading guilty was no apology. And yet, there was a sense of satisfaction to it all. They had won a battle. They had righted a grievous wrong and sent a child molester to jail. But, Molly thought, they would not win the war until they succeeded in convincing others to be open and honest by reporting sexual criminals to the police—even if these criminals attended church on a regular basis and had become their friends.

Molly had the sudden urge to plant a tree—like Grandpa Feldman did to celebrate special occasions. She decided that the day after the sentencing they would plant one, whatever Ted chose, to symbolize growth, new life, and an upward direction. If the therapy reimbursement money came through, they could take a vacation and legally change the spelling of their name to Broker.

And then the brilliance of her happiness faded as she silently stood to her feet and walked toward the stairs to Ted's room to tell him the news: Lloyd's sentence would probably require him to serve only six months in jail. Ted and Steve knew that their own sentences—as victims—would last a lifetime. The lives of their whole family would continue to be a series of challenges, the focus of which they would never have chosen. Yet, their experience had revealed that they possessed an amazing strength of which they might not have otherwise been aware. With professional help and through learning to trust, they could look forward to the best revenge of all: a happy life.

Epilogue

The sentencing took place at the end of October in a fairly large courtroom at the county courthouse. After the prosecuting attorney had presented his case, asking for six months in jail and five years' probation, he told the judge that Steve and Molly had a statement to make.

Together they outlined the extent of Lloyd's molestations and told of the pain they had endured both directly because of the molestation and in their attempt to end it by bringing the matter to the justice system.

When they sat down, the defense attorney painted a picture of a wonderful, cooperative man, pointing out that Lloyd had been in therapy and had not recently molested. He asked for a work-release program instead of jail.

Then it was Lloyd's turn. He stood and uttered the words Molly thought she would never hear: "My name is Lloyd Bowker, and I am a pedophile." He went on to claim that because of therapy, he now knew the warning signs of when he was "at risk," and said he was sure he wouldn't molest again.

When he was finished, the judge handed down the sentence: twenty years in prison for rape, ten years for indecent liberties, to be served concurrently. But the judge went on to say that he was suspending the sentence and requiring Lloyd to serve 180 days in the work-release program, with five years of therapy and continued probation. Lloyd was required to stay away from children and never to be alone either inside or outside his house.

Looking at Steve and Molly, the judge said, "I wish the laws of this state were harsher, but I must follow the laws that have been established for sentencing of this crime." Then, turning to Lloyd again, he continued, "Let me assure you that any violation at all of your sentence will result in immediate revocation of the suspension, and you will serve the full sentence in prison."

Ted heard the sentence with a grim set to his mouth. At the sound of the judge's gavel, he whispered to Molly, "That's not justice! This criminal system is insane. If I assaulted that jerk, I'd get three years in jail—and look what he gets for fifty years of hurting kids!"

They left the courtroom feeling they had accomplished little except for getting Lloyd's name and DNA type permanently registered on the statewide sexual offender list and putting a crimp in his schedule and sleeping arrangements. Later, confirming their feelings, Aunt Vera informed them that Lloyd cheerfully said of his sentence: "On work release, I just sleep in an army-type bunker at night and go to work in the morning. I can even have my sentence shortened a couple of months by good behavior! It's not going to be bad at all. When it's done, life will be pretty much back to normal."

. . . .

Because this is a true story, its ending doesn't tie up neatly. The struggles continue. Ted is doing well in college, but is still battling his anger. He didn't become a skinhead, but instead considers himself a Christian and attends church—though at this point he feels no need of formally joining a denomination.

Steve and Molly have joined a group of parents whose children were victims of abuse to lobby for stricter laws on child molesters. They also hope their story will lead to a change in the Christian community's attitude toward the crime of sex abuse and the church's treatment of child molesters.

Lloyd's church continues to deny that he is dangerous, but his therapist predicts that he will molest again.

What You Can Do:
A Counselor's Comments

by Carol Cannon*

This narrative, though extremely well-written, is difficult to read. The events described are unspeakable. The anguish of the victims, the horror of the crime, the utter naiveté of those who were aware of the problem and could have intervened, are incomprehensible.

Unfortunately, the sexual victimization of children is not uncommon. According to current data from the U.S. Department of Justice, one in three girls and one in seven boys will be sexually molested—robbed of their innocence—before the age of eighteen.[1] How often does this problem occur within the church? We don't really know. Some experts suggest that the incidence is higher in fundamentalist churches than among the rest of the population.

The act of sexually abusing a child is not usually an isolated incident brought about by a temporary lapse in the abuser's judgment. It is a highly repetitive, compulsive behavior—an addiction as well as a criminal offense. Our society is suffused with addiction and the suffering that accompanies it. Addiction is both a moral sin and a physical disease. Unfortunately, it also tends to be transgenerational, cycling from one generation to the next. A significant percentage of males who were sexually abused as children become offenders as adults, and many women

---

* Carol Cannon, M.A., N.C.A.D.C., is clinical director and therapist at The Bridge, a Christian center for treating dependency disorders in Bowling Green, Kentucky.

who were offended as children become chronic victims or marry sexual abusers.

The fact that pedophilia is an illness does not make it any less painful to the victims, nor does it excuse the crime. The offenders' defect of character may have been programmed into them by childhood trauma, but it is their responsibility to get help so that innocent children don't suffer.

People who offend children sexually are out of control. They cannot will to behave differently, because their wills are damaged. Someone has to force them to stop. The tragedy is that few Christians understand addiction, particularly sexual addiction. They either deny its existence or avoid appropriate confrontation. In doing so, they unwittingly help addicts stay sick. To the extent that they allow themselves to remain uninformed, they become part of the pathology.

I urge readers to use the feelings generated by this story to motivate themselves to action. Weep. Pray. Then educate yourself: The Saviour gave His precious life in order to establish a church capable of caring for both victims and victimizers.

How to identify the vulnerable

Who is susceptible to sexual abuse? Any trusting, obedient child may be at risk, but neglected, under-nurtured, emotionally deprived children who have strong needs for attention and affir-mation seem to be the most vulnerable. As one sexual offender put it, "A boy who isn't getting the affection and recognition he craves is at greatest risk." Youngsters who have an emotional need for a friend are most easily controlled.[2] Children who are alienated and isolated are likely to be targeted.

Parents must discuss sexuality with their children. A pedophile who victimized hundreds of children made this statement: "I made advances, yes, but I never forced myself on a boy." Children are not deaf, dumb, and blind, he said. They are aware of innuendo, dirty jokes, overt sexuality. "Parents have themselves to blame if their sons haven't learned the values and morals they need to say No to a man like me."[3]

How to prevent child sexual abuse

Short of handcuffing yourself to your children, you probably can't guard them closely enough to guarantee that they will never be sexually abused. Such offenses can occur swiftly and subtly. Children have been sexually abused in the same house with their parents, even in the same room or the same car—when help was just a scream away. Since you can't provide complete protection, you can best help them by equipping them to protect themselves.

The first preventive measure I would suggest is this: Treat your children respectfully so that they will know they have rights and will be able to assert them. Children who are maltreated lose their God-given sense of value. They don't see themselves as deserving of respect and so become more vulnerable to abuse.

Don't disempower your children, don't disallow their feelings, don't insist that they be needless and wantless, don't expect them to be so selfless that they are rendered boundary-less (unable to set limits). Don't rob them of individuality, identity, ego-strength. Children thus disempowered feel they have neither the right nor the ability to protect themselves.

In addition, tell your children explicitly what sexual abuse is. Show them how to protect themselves from sexual exploitation. Telling a child to avoid strangers is not enough. More than 80 percent of sexual crimes against children are committed by friends or relatives—people who are anything but strangers.

Talking about appropriate and inappropriate touch is *safety* education, not sex education. Children must be told that no person has the right to touch their bodies in an intimate manner, not even an adult. They need to know that respecting adults does not mean blindly obeying them. They should be taught that if anyone touches them in an area their underwear (or a bathing suit) covers, they are to *run*, *yell*, and *tell*. If anyone exposes himself or herself to them or tries to force physical contact, they should go to an adult and report what happened. And they should keep telling until they are heard and protected!

Children should be taught to say No assertively: to stand tall, to speak in a strong, firm voice, and to use body language (eye contact, a stomp of the foot) to get their message across. They must be taught to continue saying No until the offensive behavior stops.

If you don't know how to go about talking over these issues with your children, check with the schools or social service agencies in your community. Most of them have free literature that shows parents and teachers how to educate children about sexual safety.

Perhaps the most important preventive measure, however, is for you to be approachable, askable. *Never* shame a child about his or her own childish sexual behavior. When your child behaves sexually—plays doctor, masturbates, etc.—treat the issue matter-of-factly. Guide without shaming. Children who associate shame with sex are unlikely to report sexual offenses because they are afraid they will be blamed.

How to detect sexual abuse

Sexual abuse can range from a single episode to years of torment. The effects vary from little or no apparent distress to disabling psychological harm: major distortion of personality, sexual anxiety, crippling phobias.

It is important for parents to be acute to subtle cues. If a child has an unusual fear of or aversion to anyone, pay attention. If the child is uneasy in someone's presence, if he or she is reluctant to be alone with a particular person or resists going to their house or riding in their car or attempts in any way to avoid anyone, take heed.

There are specific symptoms that are considered indicators of sexual abuse, but they may indicate other problems as well. Possible symptoms include hyperactivity, sleep disturbance, chronic bedwetting, disruptive behavior, difficulty concentrating, accident proneness, depression, clinging, compulsively picking at skin or pulling hair. Withdrawal, distrust, and loneliness are indicators, as are low self-esteem and deep, overriding shame. Aggression, drawing violent pictures, bullying, hurting animals, etc., are also indicators. Consciously or unconsciously, victims of sexual abuse feel anger toward their parents or guardians for failing to protect them. This may manifest itself as generalized rage or antisocial behavior.

Inappropriate sexual knowledge or sexually offensive behavior is a hallmark of abuse, as is premature involvement in boy-girl relationships or avoidance thereof. Many victims of abuse by a person of the same gender develop serious concerns about their sexual identity, assuming that they must be homosexual or the abuser would not have been attracted to them.

Drug abuse and eating disorders are common among teenagers who have been sexually offended. Other symptoms include running away, truancy, promiscuity, and compulsive cleanliness. And long-range consequences of abuse include an inability to remember large portions of childhood; efforts to be unattractive; underachievement or overachievement; difficulty with sexuality; impotence, frigidity, etc.; perfectionism; fear of marriage and parenting; depression and suicidal thoughts; compulsive victimization or abusiveness; sleep disorders; post-traumatic stress disorder; or multiple personality disorder, when the abuse has been prolonged, ritualistic, or violent.

A single symptom may not indicate that a child has been molested. If a number of symptoms are present, however, and if the child's behavior represents a sudden or dramatic change, it is important to consider the possibility.

How to respond to reported abuse

When a child reports that he or she has been abused, the parent must maintain calm, or the child may decide not to disclose information in order to spare the parent's feelings. Allow the child to talk without applying pressure. Assure the child that reporting the abuse was the right thing to do.

Believe your children. Assure them that neither the abuse nor the aftermath is their fault. Say, "I'm sorry you had a bad experience with so-and-so. What that person did was wrong. But *you* didn't do anything bad. You did the *right* thing in telling me about it." If the abuser was someone the child knows and loves, he or she might hesitate to tell to avoid getting the abuser in trouble. Assure the child that you will try to help the offender.

Do not, under any circumstances, attempt to verify the child's story or to disprove it. Don't investigate the matter, confront the perpetrator, or try to determine guilt. Don't negotiate with the offender or the offender's family. And never, never attempt to "deal" with the problem without contacting Child Protective Services! Report the abuse and leave the investigation to the authorities. For the sake of the child, do not discuss the matter with anyone but the proper authorities.

If it is confirmed that abuse has occurred, don't hesitate to prosecute the perpetrator. Prosecuting helps give autonomy back to the child. Don't explain or excuse the abuser's behavior to the child or insist that it is the child's Christian duty to forgive the abuser. To do this is to reabuse the child. It is not necessary to protect the offender's feelings or reputation. The victim's family should be concerned about the victim. Leave the offender's care to others.

If necessary, seek medical care for the child, but be very supportive in the process. Take measures to make the child comfortable and relieve his or her pain and shame during the examination. Assure the child that the abuse does not mean that he or she is in any way flawed or defective.

Psychological support is even more important than medical attention. Sexual abuse leaves invisible scars. The emotional well-being of the child must be attended to. Local Rape Crisis Prevention Centers make services available to sexual abuse victims and their families. They will provide or recommend a therapist who can help the child release his or her feelings. Byall means, allow the child to be angry. Anger is healthy. It restores the child's sense of autonomy and self-respect.

Parents of sexually abused children are secondary victims of the crime. Their needs must also be addressed. They feel guilt, remorse, rage. They need to find a confidant, someone with whom they can share their feelings. They may need to cry,tomp, scream, throw things—but not in the presence of the child. It is OK to share feelings appropriately with the child in due time. By letting him or her know they feel angry, for instance, parents demonstrate that they value the child.

Helping the abuser

Addiction does not give way to willpower. The addict is unable to control or arrest his or her addictive behavior. Somebody has to love the addict enough to confront the symptoms and insist that he or she get help. As with any other disease, the sooner the addict is treated, the better the prognosis for recovery. For the church to deny the existence of inappropriate sexual behavior or to refuse to confront it is not an act of love or mercy.

The most effective rehabilitation combines individual and group counseling, drugs that inhibit the sexual drive, and twelve-step programs similar to those used to treat alcoholism and drug dependency.[4] Nothing short of this will do. Sexual addiction is not something that can be wished or even prayed away. It requires professional help.

What about false accusations?

All states now have child abuse reporting laws. Any form of suspected child maltreatment must be reported by any professional who is aware of it. About twenty states *require* all citizens to report, and all states *allow* any citizen to report.

With the increased reporting of child sexual abuse in recent years has come an increased potential for false accusations. There have been cases in which children fabricated or embellished sexual abuse stories to please adults, get revenge against a parent or stepparent, or gain attention.[5] But it would be unwise and unfair to discredit all abuse reported by children because a few may falsely accuse. Research projects undertaken to determine how widespread the problem of false accusation actually is indicate that this syndrome is not as prevalent as has been reported by the media.[6]

Together, the professional community and the legal system have developed reliable techniques for substantiating claims and determining whether to pursue criminal charges when children relate accounts of physical or sexual abuse. As with any other crime, final determination of guilt or innocence must be made via due process.

What churches should do

The challenge for the Christian community is manyfold. We need to mediate help to individuals suffering from sexual addiction and to families affected by abuse. That is a given. By way of prevention, we must allow meaningful background checks on those entrusted with our children to ensure that we are not allowing proven pedophiles to move from church to church or school to school unhindered. Offenders are drawn to occupations where they have access to potential victims. We must deny them that access.

As church members, we must avoid falling into the timeless trap of applying simplistic formulas and pat answers to problems of sexual abuse. We must not assume that remorse, sincere promises, superficial treatment, or even imprisonment will deter the offender. Offenders don't "learn their lesson." Courts can mandate the kind of professional help sexual abusers need, and that's what it usually takes to get them into treatment.

Above all, for the sake of the afflicted *and* the affected, we need to quell our systemic compulsion to gossip when allegations are made. We should practice the golden rule in relating to all concerned—abusers, victims, and their families. We need to reserve personal judgment and leave the final verdict to the legal system and to God. There is no question that His grace is sufficient.

---

1. Ruth Miller Fitzgibbons, "Can Child Molesters Be Stopped?" *Redbook*, April 1992, 87.

2. Ross M. Nelson with Ruth Miller Fitzgibbons, "Why I'm Every Mother's Worst Fear," *Redbook*, April 1992, 86, 116. See also Finkelhor, Hotaling, Lewis, and Smith, "Sexual Abuse in a National Survey of Adult Men and Women: Prevalence, Characteristics, and Risk Factors," *Child Abuse and Neglect,* 14 (1990), 162.

3. Ibid.

4. Fitzgibbons, "Can Child Molesters Be Stopped?" 87.

5. Rosenfeld, Nadelson, and Kreiger, "Fantasy and Reality in Patients' Reports of Incest," *Journal of Clinical Psychiatry* 40 (1979), 159-164.

6. "Editor's Note," *Prosecutor's Perspective* (January 1988). See also Nancy Thoennes and Patricia Tjaden, "The Extent, Nature, and Validity of Sexual Abuse Allegations in Custody/Visitation Desputes," *Child Abuse and Neglect*, 14 (1990), 24.

Resources

Scripture

Psalm 34:18

Luke 17:1-4

Hebrews 10:26, 27

1 Peter 2:13, 14

Proverbs 24:24, 25

1 Corinthians 5:11-13

Hebrews 12:11

2 Peter 2

Ecclesiastes 8:11

Hebrews 6:4, 5

James 1:13-15

Organizations

Childhelp IOF Foresters Hot Line—Telephone: 1-800-422-4453. (You may call this organization for guidance, literature, or to report a suspected child abuse.)

National Organization for Victims' Assistance
1757 Park Road, NW
Washington, DC 20010

Survivors of Incest Anonymous. Telephone: 301-282-3400.

Publications

Bass, Ellen, and Laura Davis. *The Courage to Heal: A Guide for Women Survivors of Child Sexual Abuse.* New York: Harper-Collins, 1988. (Laura Davis has also written a workbook by the same name to use with this book. Harper Collins, 1990.)

Byerly, Carolyn M. *The Mother's Book: How to Survive the Incest of Your Child.* Dubuque, Iowa: Kendall/Hunt Publishing Co., 1992.

Forward, Susan. *Toxic Parents: Overcoming Their Hurtful*

Legacy and Reclaiming Your Life. New York: Bantam Books, 1990.

Frank, Jan. *A Door of Hope: Recognizing and Resolving the Pains of Your Past.* San Bernardino, Calif.: Here's Life Publishers, 1987.

Hindman, Jan. *A Very Touching Book.* Ontario, Oreg.: Alex-Andria Associates, 1983. (Using lighthearted illustrations to keep the discussion from becoming too threatening, this book explains child abuse to children.)

Peters, David. *A Betrayal of Innocence: What Everyone Should Know About Child Sexual Abuse.* Waco, Tex.: Word Books, 1986.

Sanford, Doris. *I Can't Talk About It: A Child's Book About Sexual Abuse.* Portland, Oreg.: Multnomah Press, 1986. (Written for children who may be victims.)

Seamands, David. *Healing for Damaged Emotions.* Wheaton, Ill.: Victor Books, 1991.

_____. *Healing of Memories.* Wheaton, Ill.: Victor Books, 1985.

Wilson, Earl D. *A Silence to Be Broken: Hope for Those Caught in the Web of Incest.* Portland, Oreg.: Multnomah Press, 1986.

Wooden, Kenneth. "How Sex Offenders Lure Our Children," *Reader's Digest.* June 1988, 149.

Audiotape
Fast, Stephanie. "Healing Childhood Traumas." Focus on the Family, Colorado Springs, Colo. (This is Stephanie's life story.)